A BETTER WAY

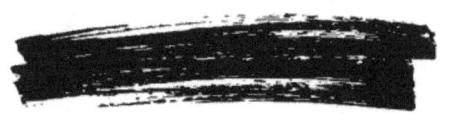

Novel adaptation by
Alison Miller

Adapted from the Screenplay,
A Better Way,
by **Erik V Wolter**

A Better Way
Copyright ©2025 Dalas L. Davis

ISBN 978-1506-915-43-2 PBK

October 2025

Published and Distributed by
First Edition Design Publishing, Inc.
P.O. Box 17646, Sarasota, FL 34276-3217
www.firsteditiondesignpublishing.com

ALL RIGHTS RESERVED. No part of this book publication may be reproduced, stored in a retrieval system, or transmitted in any form or by any means — electronic, mechanical, photocopy, recording, or any other — except brief quotation in reviews, without the prior permission of the author or publisher.

CHAPTER ONE

Seventeen-year-old Casey Henderson held a hanger against her chest, eyeing the new outfit in her bedroom mirror. She moved this way and that, tilted her head from side to side, tried to imagine herself dressed and ready to go out later that evening. Her friend Sophia Garcia, who was sprawled out on Casey's floral bedspread scrolling through her phone, paid no attention to Casey. Instead, she watched dance videos. A familiar song played over the speaker and Casey let the beat of the music flood her body as she swayed in front of the mirror. She considered her dilemma: Should she wear this outfit, which was edgier than her usual attire but not completely inappropriate, or take it to the next level and wear something undeniably sexy and sure to get her some looks?

Tonight's event was a big deal—like a really huge deal that she was lucky even to have been invited to. Not just anyone got an invitation but being friends with Chantel Jackson had its perks. Casey and Chantel had been friends since forever, even before Chantel had her huge social media following. Casey had been there in the beginning, when Chantel first started her online account and posted her first dance video. She had watched in awe as Chantel grew her following in a short amount of time by posting videos of her creative dance moves. Everyone loved Chantel and wanted to emulate her. She was an incredible dancer, smart, sexy, and confident. Casey would be lying if she didn't admit she envied those qualities.

Last week when Chantel invited Casey, she had told her to bring a guest. "Just make sure you both cheer for me," Chantel had said, half joking, half serious. She was referencing the main event of the night, the Dance 4 Cash competition that would take place center stage. A lot of money would be up for grabs and Chantel was the favorite to win. Of course, she didn't need Casey's or Sophia's cheers to tip the votes, she was always the best dancer. Another win was expected.

Casey felt excitement in her stomach as she thought about later that night. She and Sophia would join a ton of local dancers, social media influencers, and fans at a warehouse near downtown Orlando and dance the night away. Casey had her own social media platform but it wasn't anything near Chantel's. Casey wanted tonight to be an image reset of sorts, a way to grow her following and be more like Chantel.

She took one last look at the outfit in the mirror. She had loved it when she bought it earlier at the cute vintage shop around the corner from school. She and Sophia had grabbed coffee at their favorite cafe after classes and then dashed inside the shop for a quick look. Just a quick look, Casey had told herself, because she knew she shouldn't be buying anything new, especially if it wasn't something her mother would fully approve of. Casey sighed and made a face at her reflection. She was seventeen, old enough to decide what to wear without needing her mother's permission.

As she headed for her closet to change, she picked up some plastic wrap from the floor and placed it in the small trash bin beside her desk. She saw a tiny piece of lint on her pillowcase so she picked that up too and threw it away. She took a moment to smooth out the pastel frilly pillowcase and then straighten the picture frame on her nightstand. Sophia had grabbed it earlier to look at.

That particular picture was one of Casey's favorites from her childhood. It was taken on a Sunday, after church, a rare day when her family went out for an ice cream treat after services. Casey sat next to her mother on an old rotted log at the city park. She was around seven years old, missing a front tooth but smiling as big as the sky anyway. Her blonde hair was long even back then but messy. In the picture, Casey, gazing upwards towards her mom's face, had chocolate ice cream smeared all over her mouth and chin. Some had dribbled down her shirt. Her mom, who was looking directly at the camera, also had a huge smile. It was a happy moment. And even though Casey's father wasn't in the picture, he was the one behind the camera that day, back when they were still a family.

Casey shook the familiar sadness at the thought of happier times from her mind. She glanced at the framed picture of Jesus hanging over her bed and steeled herself against the past. She distracted herself with mulling over the decision about the outfit. As she headed into the closet to change, she said, "I'll be out in a sec," to Sophia, who was still absorbed in watching videos. As Casey shut the closet door, she heard Chantel's voice on one of the videos talking about something wonderful in her perfect life.

CHAPTER TWO

Casey's walk-in closet was roomy and neatly organized. Clothes hung in an orderly fashion on matching plastic hangers from the rods, grouped by type and color. Her jeans were neatly folded on pants hangers and lined up on the bottom rod. Her T-shirts and blouses, all ironed and carefully arranged, hung above the pants. Dresses and skirts hung on the right side of the center tower system that housed five drawers on the bottom section and five shelves on the upper section. The drawers were where she stored essentials like undergarments, socks, and workout clothes. She kept a lighted makeup mirror, a pink makeup caddy, and assorted lotions and nail polish on the first shelf that doubled as a vanity table. The clear plastic boxes neatly stacked on the top wire rack that ran the length of the closet were for shoes, mementos, extra items she didn't need every day. She didn't like to store clutter on the floor if she didn't have to.

She changed into the outfit and touched up her makeup before taking a deep breath and strolling out of the closet. Unsurprisingly Sophia was still sprawled out on the bed looking through videos. Casey wondered how her body hadn't gone numb yet from non-movement. She shook her head in disbelief, though she wasn't truly annoyed with Sophia. She understood how mesmerizing Chantel's and all the dance videos could be. How many times had she herself thought she'd watch one or two videos but found herself an hour later still watching?

She stood in front of the mirror again, this time wearing the new outfit, and scrutinized her appearance. Cute, yes, but stylish? She wasn't sure. She liked the jean skirt but beyond being shorter than her usual skirts, there was nothing especially eye-catching about it. And the top, though it showed a sliver of her belly when she raised her arms, was plain and too loose.

"Well?" she said to Sophia's reflection.

Sophia rolled over and sat up on the bed, her feet dangling off the side. She gave Casey the once over, made a face, and shook her head. She then rolled back onto her stomach and resumed watching videos. Casey shrugged and marched back into the walk-in closet.

About ten minutes later Casey emerged from the closet wearing a shorter skirt, a form-fitting sweater, and wedge heels. She had touched up her makeup and tied her long blonde hair into a smooth top bun. She sauntered over to the mirror and took in this current outfit. She nodded, pleased with the way she looked. This outfit definitely had a sexy vibe going on, but the more she looked at herself reflected, the more she felt unsure. Would it be enough to get her the attention—and followers—she wanted? Even though it was way sexier than anything she would normally wear, it wasn't close to being as sexy as the one Chantel had suggested she wear.

"Hey, Sophia!" Casey said, striking a pose in front of her friend.

Startled by the sudden call out, Sophia glanced up at Casey and her entire face went into shock, eyes wide, mouth slightly agape.

"Seriously, Casey?" she said shaking her head in disbelief. "Come on now." She closed her eyes and pointed to the closet. "Go!"

Casey laughed at her friend's reaction, but before she returned to the closet for yet another outfit change, she peeked at Sophia's phone screen. Chantel was doing one of her signature dances, dancing the way she danced best: steamy sexy, fluid moves. Dang, she was soooo good at dancing. Casey wanted to be that good and look as good doing it too.

A Better Way

She watched Chantel's video for a moment. Chantel wore short shorts paired with a bikini top. She was doing her version of one of the popular trend dances. Casey began to move with the music, tried to mimic Chantel's choreography. There was a reason Chantel Jackson had almost a million and a half followers: she was phenomenal.

Back in the closet, Casey perused her clothes for options. After watching that last video of Chantel, she wasn't feeling love for this current outfit. It may have shocked Sophia but her new friend wasn't someone who took risks with her outfits. She had on baggy jeans, sneakers, and a basic top for the event that night.

Casey knew Chantel would be dressed to impress tonight, full makeup and hair done. Chantel didn't go anywhere without looking like the best version of her brand image.

That image had changed over the last couple of years too. Chantel used to dress less . . . provocative, but always had a nice style. Who Chantel was now wasn't who she was two years ago. If her friend could transform her style then couldn't Casey do the same thing? She didn't have to be locked into the cute good girl style she'd always had. Whose style was that anyway? Hers or her mother's?

From one of the bottom drawers, Casey pulled out a skirt and top she had bought while shopping months ago with Chantel, who had joked that if Casey didn't buy it she couldn't be Chantel's friend anymore. Casey had never had the nerve to wear it out in public, and kept it hidden in the bottom drawer under a pile of other clothes in case her mother ever happened to snoop—not that her mother ever did that, but there was a first for everything. Casey didn't want to justify her clothing choices. That reminded her, her mother had texted a while ago from the hospital, where she worked as a nurse, letting her know she had been called in early for an emergency. *Dinner in the frig.* She had also wanted to know how Casey's job search was going. Casey groaned and sent a quick text thanking her mom for the food. She brushed off the job question. The truth was she hoped to grow her social media platform and make money off that. Chantel made a lot of money on her platform and Casey hoped she could too.

She loved to dance and though she wasn't as good as Chantel yet, she could get better. She just needed to practice and find a way to grow her following.

With the outfit from the bottom drawer in her hand, her mind swirled with conflicting thoughts. She knew her mother wouldn't approve, but her mother wouldn't be around to see her. Tonight was a huge opportunity to get in front of the right people. In addition to Chantel and other local dancers being there, there was a rumor that Ekandem Essiet would be there too. He was the premier dance instructor in the Orlando area. It was next to impossible to get into any of his classes because he was so popular. Casey had tried a couple times to sign up but basically he was booked months in advance and unless you knew someone who knew someone you weren't getting in.

She held the outfit up to get a better look. Would it hurt to try out a new style? She could always change her mind and go back to her boring clothes and boring style. Probably never get her platform off the ground but at least that was always an option.

After a lengthy back of forth with herself Casey made the decision. She updated her makeup look to match the vibe of her outfit and told herself, *Deep breaths, you've got this.*

She emerged from the closet like a top model during New York Fashion Week and catwalked her way past the bed to the center of the room where she did a pivot to face Sophia. Her friend did a double take, dropped her phone, sat up, eyes wide and mouth slightly agape.

Now that's more like it, Casey thought, reveling in her friend's reaction. Casey pivoted again and stepped in front of the mirror. She took one look at her sexy reflection and couldn't believe it was her. This ensemble was definitely the show stopper she had been going for. The postage stamp skirt showed off her toned legs while the top—very low-cut and cropped—showed off her midriff and cleavage. Her makeup was thick and dramatic. The smoky eyeshadow, lush eyelashes, and plumping lip gloss made a statement. Her long hair was now sleek and straight with side-swept bangs that covered one eye. This hairstyle reminded her of that one time in middle school, during the pandemic, when she DIY'd her own bangs because that's what everyone was doing on TikTok. Her mother had been so upset when she saw the choppy, uneven results that she demanded Casey let her fix them. "I don't like the way they hang in your eyes. You can't see where you're going!" her mom had said.

Casey shook the memory out of her mind and refocused on her appearance. She looked much older now, maybe twenty-something, definitely not a seventeen-year-old. She caught Sophia gawking at her in the reflection of the mirror and that made Casey smile with satisfaction. All it took was the right outfit and makeup to make her friend sit up and take notice.

Casey worked it for her audience of one, posing one way and then another, strutting around her room. Sophia finally closed her eyes, as if she was trying to make Casey's outfit disappear. When she opened them again, she cringed.

"Don't say it. This is the new me," Casey said. She turned back to the mirror, turned sideways and sucked in her gut. She wasn't used to showing so much of her body. In the reflection she noticed Sophia had picked up a pillow and was shaking it from its case. She turned to get a better look and was about to ask why she was messing up her neatly made bed, when the pillow-innards fell out. With the pillowcase now free, Sophia stood up on the bed. Casey gave her friend a quizzical look that asked exactly what she was wondering: *what are you doing?* In return, Sophia gave Casey a full up and down look that said exactly what she was thinking: *that outfit was a problem.* Then, one swift maneuver toward the headboard, Sophia draped the pillowcase over the portrait of Jesus hanging above the bed.

Casey narrowed her eyes, crossed her arms, and huffed. "Not funny."

Sophia plopped back down on the bed, her expression serious. "Not supposed to be."

Casey felt the disapproval of her friend's eyes on her. Her resolve softened some though as she tried to explain her reasons. "I have to get my numbers up. Chantel said—"

"You want to be like her?"

Casey shrugged. "What's wrong with that? She has over a million followers."

Sophia pressed her lips together, as if to say so what. Casey was beginning to feel exposed standing there in her skin-bearing outfit. She hugged her crossed arms tighter over her chest. "And she's been my best friend forever," she added, as if that explained everything.

Sophia had grabbed her phone off the bed and scrolled around until she quickly found what she was looking for. "One million, two hundred fifty three thousand, six hundred seventy one," she said matter-of-factly.

"What?" The numbers didn't compute for Casey.

Sophia waved her off. "Nothing. Ready to go?"

"A minute," Casey said. She checked her appearance one more time in the mirror. She was relieved Sophia wasn't going to make any bigger deal about the outfit. It didn't matter anyway, did it? She had made up her mind. She was going to wear it out tonight. She wanted to see if it actually made a difference, if maybe Chantel was right and that she needed to project a sexier image. She glanced at the pillowcase now covering Jesus and felt a small knot of uncertainty, or maybe humility, fill her. She had to turn away to make the feeling go away.

She needed reassurance and Sophia wasn't helping. She grabbed her bag off her desk and pulled out her phone. If she really wanted to grow her followers she might as well start now. She set up the phone to record, chose the music, and handed it to Sophia.

"Please?" She smiled as sweetly as possible at her friend. "I want to post this before we go."

Sophia took the phone and gave a half smile. "You better introduce yourself. No way they'll know who you are."

Casey chuckled and playfully stuck out her tongue. She actually liked the idea of no one knowing her—as her old self. She realized that she had an opportunity to become someone else, someone like Chantel, and she was going to take it.

Sophia held the phone up while Casey got into position. Sophia nodded and Casey began her monologue.

"Hi guys. Thought I would say hi before I go out tonight with my new good friend, Sophia. We're going to an underground dance contest! Can't tell you much more than that now. It's top secret. I'm not in it, but next time..."

Casey broke out into a few dance steps. She tried to incorporate some of the moves she had seen Chantel use earlier on the video. She danced for a short time before stopping and looking directly into the camera and said, "What do you think? Drop me some comments, okay? Til next time..."

Sophia hit the stop recording button and handed the phone back to Casey. "Let's go."

"Wait a minute! Let's watch it." Casey quickly uploaded the video to her Instagram account and pressed play. She was excited but anxious to hear what her fans had to say about her outfit and dance routine. She had over two hundred thousand followers and loved connecting with them. Most of their comments were supportive but there were always the haters. Chantel had told her to ignore them, which she did most of the time, but sometimes that was hard to do.

Sophia snatched Casey's phone and turned it off. She tugged at Casey's arm. "We're late. Watch it in the car."

As they headed for the door, Casey noticed the bedspread was messy where Sophia had been camped out all afternoon. She stopped and straightened it by running her hands over the lumps and tugging at the edges. Casey was naturally neat and organized. It wasn't that it just annoyed her when things were messy and out of place, it nagged at her until she put it right. She could either do a quick sweep of her room now—so she could enjoy her time out—or leave and have it bother her all night long.

Casey surveyed the rest of her room. One wall had posters of dancers she admired plastered all over it. The opposite wall held family and school pictures. She particularly loved the twine line with photo-booth style pictures of Chantel and her clipped to it. Different frames, different poses. Their expressions ranged from sexy to goofy to serious.

She zeroed in on her desk, taking a quick assessment. Laptop, stack of textbooks, a bible. Next to the bible was a pad of paper and a pen and pencil. She zoomed in on the writing utensils. She sensed Sophia getting impatient, but it would take just a moment to put things perfectly in their place.

She wiped the non-existent dust off the top of her closed laptop, straightened the bible, and rearranged the pen and pencil to be in the exact same spot—only neater. She smiled. She knew what she was doing. When she was nervous about something she became hypersensitive to clutter. She could stay here all night and micro-clean her room if she wasn't careful.

Satisfied with the way her desk looked, she took a deep breath and headed back to the exit. She wrapped her arm around Sophia's shoulder, a genuine gesture to show her friend some camaraderie. She flipped off the bedroom light and led them out. As they headed down the stairs, Sophia said, "Did you mean what you said? About me, I mean?"

Casey said, "Being my good friend? Of course . . ." But a little voice that sounded a lot like Chantel's poked her mind and she added, "Not!" She burst out laughing, expecting Sophia to laugh, too, but Sophia frowned and looked genuinely hurt.

Casey elbowed her. "I'm kidding! . . . Yes, I meant it." She gave Sophia a hug and linked her arm through her friend's as they walked through the house, toward the front door. Though she didn't say it out loud, Casey was glad Sophia was going to the dance competition with her. She *was* a friend, and now that Chantel was always so busy, Casey had started to do more with Sophia.

She had met Sophia in fourth period Stats class. Sophia's family had recently moved to Orlando and this was her first year at the high school. Casey remembered how scared and disoriented Sophia had looked on her first day. Their high school was big, over three thousand students. Lunch was scheduled after Stats so Casey asked Sophia to sit with her. Since grade school, when one of her teachers appointed her the class ambassador to all new students, Casey made it a point to be friendly and welcoming. She had never been the new kid in school but imagined how lonely it must have felt to walk into a new place and not know one single person.

A Better Way

Casey would never forget the look on Chantel's face during that lunch period when she showed up with Sophia. Not exactly angry but visibly annoyed. It had surprised Casey. She had expected Chantel to be friendly, but her old friend mostly ignored her new friend and spent their entire lunch talking about how many followers she had on social media.

Casey still considered Chantel her best friend. They had a history together; met when both had been cast in the Little Mermaid in middle school, with Chantel being Ariel, of course. She and Casey had hit it off instantly and became best friends before opening night of the musical.

It was hard to believe that just a few years ago she and Chantel had started their social media accounts at the same time. They had challenged each other to see who could get the first one hundred followers—Chantel won, and then overnight her platform took off while Casey's stayed stagnant.

As the two girls headed out of the house, looking forward to what was sure to be a memorable night, Sophia gasped and said, "Oh! I almost forgot to show you!" She pulled out her phone from her back pocket, unlocked it, and scrolled to something she had bookmarked earlier.

Casey stared at the video featuring a very handsome, very fit African American guy dancing. "Oh my God . . ." she said, as both girls watched, mesmerized by Marquis Evans and his captivating dance routine. They watched as he put his own unique style to familiar moves. He was amazing and good looking, but didn't even know Casey existed. "Chantel so wants him," Casey said, more as a reminder to herself that he was off limits anyway rather than as gossip for Sophia.

"And you?" Sophia asked.

"Me?" Casey said, trying to feign confusion.

"He sure is hot," Sophia said, smiling at Casey with a knowing look.

Casey felt a grin spread across her face. She laughed and jokingly pushed Sophia out of the house. She flipped the porch light on for her mom, locked the door, and headed out to what she knew would be a great night.

CHAPTER THREE

The Florida night air was sticky warm. Casey thought about Marquis Evans on the walk from the parked car to the warehouse where the dance competition would be held and wondered if he would be there tonight. If he was, she doubted he would notice her. The beat of hip hop music thrummed louder the closer the girls got to the club.

The warehouse parking lot buzzed with activity. People were mingling and laughter could be heard. Casey and Sophia weaved their way in and out of cars and groups of people. The excitement of the crowd was palpable. Casey saw the looks she got as she passed groups of guys and girls. One guy jumped in front of her and started walking backwards while checking her out. Sophia grabbed her hand and pulled her off into another direction, leaving the guy to throw up his hands like they had offended him. The girls laughed and ran between two cars while they continued weaving their way to the entrance of the club.

Parked in a semi-circle in part of the parking lot was a line of exotic cars. They were the most expensive cars Casey had ever seen. Her eyes caught sight of a metallic blue sports car. She had no idea what type of car it was but she loved the way it looked, its doors raised upward instead of outward.

They finally made their way to the front of the building and took their place at the end of the line waiting with everyone else for access to the club.

A Better Way

Fifty years ago, if Casey and Sophia had stepped into this space they would have been looking at a wall of giant storage bins filled to the top with Florida oranges. They would have heard the whir of the conveyor belts that transported the fruit to the juice extraction machines. They would have been intoxicated by the sweet bright smell of citrus. Originally a processing plant for frozen orange juice, the several-times-over repurposed warehouse was now the venue for the underground dance competition.

The girls were thrust into an expansive industrial room filled to the walls with people. Loud, thumping music pulsed through large speakers set up around the perimeter. A burnt staleness permeated the air but also hints of perfume and sweat.

Casey pulled Sophia over to the side so they could get their bearings and be out of the way of the people entering behind them. Sophia gripped her phone like a life raft in the sea of people swarming in. Casey took in the scenery, while also searching for anyone she might know, her mind stubbornly prodded her with an image of Marquis Evans. She was sure he was dancing in the competition tonight.

The atmosphere hummed with energy. The loud music engulfed them. Casey could feel the bass in her chest rattling around her ribcage. Flashing neon pink, blue, and green lights burned through the hazy fog, which must have been machine generated and the source of the burnt stale smell. Disco balls and a banner with the Dance 4 Cash logo hung from the rafters.

As they posed together for a selfie, a couple of older guys walked past and gave Casey's outfit a once-over. The guy wearing a ball cap had a hungry look in his eyes. His friend said something lewd that made them both laugh. They walked off without another word, leaving Casey and Sophia huddled together against the wall.

People streamed in continuously, filling the large open space. The vibe of some of these guys weren't good. She realized dressing sexy on video was completely different than being dressed like this in public. She felt exposed, not prepared for the attention she was getting.

Eventually, the two girls pushed their way through the crowd, slowly working toward the main area where the dance competition would be held. A semi-circle of onlookers three rows deep had formed at the edge of the marked off area in hopes for a good view of the competition and their favorite dancers. Casey grabbed Sophia's hand to prevent getting separated, and somehow managed to squeeze them closer so they were one row back from the action. From this spot she could see the competitors lined up and facing the crowd.

She instantly spotted Chantel in the middle of the group and tried to get her friend's attention by shouting her name and waving. Chantel didn't even look her way. The music was too loud for one thing, but Chantel was also talking to someone next to her. When Casey recognized who it was her stomach did a flip flop. Marquis Evans.

Josh, the DJ in charge of the event, came out and worked the crowd for several minutes, eventually saying, "Okay. Enough about me. But if you want more, follow me at Josh on TikTok and YouTube. We have a special guest tonight."

The roar of approval swelled from the crowd. Casey and Sophia hooted and clapped along as a guy from somewhere behind them emerged into the center of the dance floor and started to dance. He wore an oversized hoodie that covered his face and made his identity a mystery. Casey had no idea who he was but the crowd sure loved him. His moves were good, and Casey felt herself moving along to the sound of the music as she watched the mysterious dancer. Josh, always attempting to make the crowd laugh, tried to follow along but wasn't able to figure out the moves. The crowd loved it though. The guy in the hoodie entertained them for several minutes, until the music abruptly stopped, and he stood there opened stance, arms crossed. As everyone grew impatient and their murmuring grew louder, the guy pulled down his hood.

An audible gasp rippled over the crowd, followed by shouts, whistles, and claps as everyone recognized the dancer: Ekandem Essiet.

A Better Way

Casey's stomach did another flip flop. She grabbed Sophia's arm, pulled her close, and shouted, "OMG! I don't believe it!"

Josh said, "Wow. I guess you don't need much introduction. Anyway, Ekandem Essiet is here to help us out tonight with the Dance 4 Cash Finals."

Ekandem nodded his head and said, "Thanks, Josh. I'll be handing out the prize money, but it's you . . ." He gestured to the crowd, "all of you who decide who the winner is. So, when it's time, give us all the noise you got."

The crowd grew louder again but Josh made a settle-down gesture with his hand. "Okay, remember it can be a solo dancer." He pointed to Ekandem, who on cue broke into a dance routine.

Casey watched in awe as the talented choreographer showcased his musicality and foundation dance moves to create his signature style. His movements were intentional and synced with the beat of the music. When, the high energy performance came to an end, the crowd roared with applause. From the medley of noise a voice could be heard shouting, "He wins! Game over!" This brought an even louder reaction from the enthusiastic crowd.

"No way," Josh shot back at the voice. He appeared center stage, made a funny face that made everyone laugh. Next he held up two fingers and offered instructions for a partner round. He took a few steps back and gave Ekandem the spotlight.

Casey glanced at the line of competitors, who all looked confident, especially Chantel. Casey wanted to be up there so badly, but knew she wasn't ready. She saw Chantel lean over and whisper something to Marquis, and found herself pushing closer to the dance area. She mostly wanted to be up close to study Ekandem's dance moves. It was the only way she'd get better. Study and practice. There was a part of her, too, that wanted to catch Chantel's eye.

Ekandem and Josh played up the crowd, creating anticipation for the next dance. Ekandem eyed Josh, pretending like he wanted to pick him for his partner. Josh acted excited and hopeful, but then disappointed and hurt when Ekandem shook his head and waved him away.

Ekandem turned his attention to the cheering crowd. Hands went up as everyone vied for the coveted chance to be his partner.

Ekandem scanned the crowd several times, his sight unexpectedly landing on Casey. He smiled and pointed at her. Instantly, her stomach did a triple flip. *He can't mean me,* she thought. But he held out his hand. Sophia had to nudge her into motion. Suddenly she stood on the dance floor with Ekandem Essiet. *Oh my god, Ekandem Essiet,* she thought as she gave him the biggest, cheesiest smile she had ever given anyone.

She took a second to glance toward the line of competitors and saw Chantel's surprised but unimpressed look. Even Marquis, who didn't know she existed, had his eyes on her. All that attention made her nervous. She hoped she didn't screw up, not in front of Marquis and especially not in front of Chantel. She glanced at Sophia who had her phone up, recording. She gave Casey a nod and thumbs up.

As the music started, Ekandem leaned in and whispered, "Just follow me."

Casey adjusted her micro-mini skirt and tiny top and hoped that her clothes would stay in place as she danced. Ekandem counted them in and the dance started. Following his lead, Casey mimicked his steps the best she could. She let the music take over her movements and tried to have fun as she and Ekandem danced as partners in front of the large crowd. It wasn't a long routine, thank goodness, but it allowed her to showcase her abilities. Applause and cheers erupted when they were finished. Though Casey knew she had messed up a couple steps, the reception of the crowd reassured her.

As she left the floor she heard someone from behind her yell, "Nice work, Casey!" She turned to see who said it and Marquis Evans was looking right at her with a smile. Her face flushed. She didn't think he even knew her name! And now he was calling her out by her name, telling her she had done good. That meant a lot coming from him, since he was an excellent dancer himself. Chantel turned and gave him a look that said something like *you can't be serious*, and then totally snubbed Casey. *Ouch*, Casey thought.

But she was still riding high from her moment on the dance floor. She quickly stepped back into the crowd next to Sophia.

"Oh my God . . . Oh my God! Did that really happen?"

Sophia gave her a hug and told her she had done a great job. Casey felt her body start to shake as all the tension from the moment released. She'd never forget it.

She was barely paying attention to anything else going on around her now. She kept stealing glances toward Marquis, who was stealing glances at her. She wanted to squeal with excitement but needed to keep her cool.

Josh was back on center stage. "It can be any kind of dance," he announced. Ekandem nodded and this time pointed to Sophia. He motioned for her to come stand next to him. Sophia gave Casey a wide-eyed look. Neither of them could believe this was happening a second time to them. Sophia seemed frozen in place so Casey pushed her out onto the dance floor. She walked hesitantly over to Ekandem as the crowd roared with excitement. Casey set her phone to record as the two prepared to dance.

Ekandem whispered something to Sophia to which Sophia responded with something. He nodded and she smiled as they faced each other in a closed position embrace, a few inches separating their bodies, his left hand holding her right. The neon lights flickered bright as lively fast tempo music blared from the speakers. Ekandem commanded the lead and swept Sophia into the rhythmic steps of merengue. As Sophia loosened up, Ekandem led her into turns. The crowd loved the fun, energetic dance.

Once they were finished with the short routine, Sophia rejoined Casey in the crowd.

Back on stage Josh said, "Okay. Let's do this! First up!"

As the music cranked up again, the lights flashed like lasers and the bass vibrated the floor. The crowd pressed in tighter so everyone could get a better look. Chantel took center spotlight, energized, every eye in the room drawn to her.

She swayed her hips, her body rolling effortlessly to the rhythm of the club mix. Casey watched in awe and admiration as Chantel made every hip rock precise, every pause deliberate. She wasn't just following the beat, she owned it. Her confidence radiated off her like steam. On the dance floor, Chantel was bold and unapologetic.

Then came Marquis's turn. His movements hit harder, each step landing with intention. He channeled power and control as he took charge of the dance floor. Casey couldn't take her eyes off him. She loved the way he moved.

Chantel took center spotlight again and became fire—seductive, sinuous, spellbinding. Marcus took over and became thunder—fierce, commanding, intense.

Their performances wowed the crowd.

After the last dance, Josh reappeared on the stage.

"Thanks to all of you for coming tonight. Remember now. I know you all want to follow me, so it's Josh on TikTok and on YouTube it's —"

Ekandem dashed out and whispered something in his ear.

"Oh right. Don't forget to follow Ekandem on . . ."

Ekandem playfully pushed Josh and said, "That's not what I said!"

"No, but you wanted to. Right? Truth now."

Ekandem folded his arms across his chest and shook his head.

"Okay, truth is he didn't say that. But only because he doesn't need any more followers. But the rest of us . . ."

The crowd roared with laughter as Ekandem chased him around in a circle, like this was a rehearsed comedy sketch. After a couple rounds of chase, Ekandem stopped in the center and made a gesture to indicate they would be serious now. "So, it's time we decide the winner. How much cash do we have, Mr. TikTok, YouTube, Instagram . . . Sir?"

Josh laughed at the Ekandem's joke. He held up an envelope of money and said, "We have $3,500 and change." The crowd broke into applause. Josh waited for it to quiet down before continuing. "And Ekandem, as a thank you for gracing us with your presence tonight with your over 12 million YouTube subscribers . . . And let's not forget your 3.8 million followers on Instagram . . . You can keep the change." Josh smiled his charming smile as he stared out at the laughing but appreciative crowd. He was a total comedian at heart. He continued, "Seriously now . . . That means I keep the change . . . " He encouraged more crowd laughter. "No really, let's hear it for our first performer! Let's hear it for Chantel Jackson!"

At the mention of her name, the music cued up and the crowd let out a thunderous roar of approval as she danced out to the center to stand beside Ekandem and Josh.

"How about Marquis Evans!" Josh shouted into the mic so the crowd could hear.

The crowd roared again as Marquis danced his way to stand beside Chantel. Off to the side Josh and Ekandem huddled together to discuss the winner. The crowd waited impatiently, clapping and shouting out their favorite dancer.

Casey couldn't take her eyes off Marquis. He looked her way every now and then, but Casey got the feeling that Chantel had said something to him about her. Chantel still didn't even acknowledge her as a friend, someone who had come out to support her.

Casey turned to Sophia and said, "I'm thinking Marquis."

"You're biased," Sophia said.

Finally, Josh and Ekandem broke from their huddle and walked to center stage again. The crowd went quiet. Everyone wanted to know the winner. Casey felt excited for her friend, though she sensed something had shifted between them earlier that night, when Casey had been called up to dance. If she were being honest, she wanted Marquis to win, but it would be easier if Chantel won. Chantel didn't take losing very well.

Josh asked for a drumroll. "Our Dance 4 Cash winner is. . ." He paused long enough to make the crowd rumble with impatience, then shouted, "Chantel Jackson!"

What had been loud cheering earlier was now deafening. People were stomping, clapping, shouting. The music blasted through the speakers. Ekandem handed Chantel the envelope of money as a cluster of admirers and friends rushed to surround Chantel. Her friend beamed with joy as she hugged the other dancers. Casey would have gone up and congratulated her but it looked impossible to penetrate that crowd of people.

She and Sophia were turning to leave when someone tapped her on the shoulder. She spun around to find Marquis Evans standing there. For the fourth time that night, her stomach did a huge flip flop.

CHAPTER

FOUR

The bedroom light flicked on. Casey's eyes burned from the sudden brightness. She clinched them shut and rubbed away the pain. When she opened them again, her mother, Kelly Henderson, was standing inside the door with her arms crossed. Still dressed in her blue hospital scrubs, she looked exhausted after the long shift in the ICU.

"A little late tonight, Casey," her mother said, scowling. Casey had fallen asleep on top of the bed covers, still dressed in her club clothes.

"Sorry, mom. I was going to call, but . . . I thought . . . You know . . ."

"No, I don't know," her mother said, eyeing her choice of outfit. Casey wished she had changed into her sweat pants and T-shirt before her mother had come home. Her mother bit her bottom lip and let out a huge sigh as if she didn't know what to say to her daughter. Finally she asked, "An underground dance contest?"

Casey's video from earlier had gained a few hundred likes already, not even close to being viral. She hadn't uploaded the videos or selfies from the dance competition yet. She wanted the dance with Ekandem to go viral so badly. "Oh, you saw my—"

"I'm not about to wait for your next video, so . . ."

In their home, one of her mother's rules was if Casey wanted a phone and access to the Internet, she had to allow her mother access to her accounts. She wasn't allowed to make anything private, and if her mother ever discovered Casey had a secret account, which Casey didn't, but if she did, her mother would be furious and take her phone privileges away.

"It's kind of hard to explain," Casey said.

"Start with the underground part."

"Mom, it's just a dance contest... But... Well, it's called Dance 4 Cash, so, you know..."

"It's illegal. You called it top secret."

"I just said that. You have to be invited, that's all. I didn't say it was illegal."

"It's late. We'll talk more tomorrow." She tapped her cell phone a couple times. "Wait. Can't. I have a double shift tomorrow at the hospital. Soon, though." Casey's mother turned to leave but paused and turned back. "So, this... Look, or whatever..." She gestured toward Casey's appearance. "This is what you want to be?"

Casey shrugged. There were a lot of things she wanted to be. She wanted to be a dancer first, but she had tried that as herself and it wasn't getting her anywhere on building a following on social media. She didn't necessarily want to go out half dressed, but it worked for Chantel, and hadn't her outfit gotten her picked out of the crowd by Ekandem? The fallacy with that argument was that Sophia had been picked too, by wearing baggy jeans, a cute top, and Nikes. She had more clothes on than most of the girls at the club. So maybe it wasn't the outfits. Perplexing. She wished she could talk to her mom about it but she didn't think her mom would understand.

Kelly's eyes shifted to above Casey's bed, landing on the Jesus portrait that Casey had forgotten to remove the pillowcase from. Her mother looked disappointed. "Why?"

"No. Mom, I didn't do that. Sophia, my new friend... She was just trying to be funny. She's new at school."

Kelly crossed her arms. "Covering up Jesus Christ is funny? We'll talk about that, too. Good night."

Without another word, her mother left. Casey felt terrible. She stood up on her bed and removed the pillowcase from the portrait. She stared at the picture of Jesus for a moment.

Back when her father was around, her family used to go to church every Sunday. Those were happier times. Her mother didn't work as much and they did more things as a family. She remembered the day her father had helped her hang up the portrait. He even let her hit the nail with the hammer a few times. That had been a good day.

CHAPTER
FIVE

Chantel Jackson had the bed covers pulled over her head, trying to block out any late morning light filtering through her closed blinds. Was it too much to ask for the stupid sun to go away? So rude of the giant fireball to interrupt her sleep. She had been up late the night before, texting and FaceTiming friends, who had wanted to congratulate her for winning the Dance 4 Cash competition. She had posted a couple videos on her Instagram account and her followers went wild over them. She planned to stay in bed longer, to relive the night and think about the first thing she'd buy with the cash. But something nagged at her; each time she came to a particular moment in last night's memories, she had to stop the playback, rewind, and replay. She kept coming to the same conclusion: Nothing cool about what he did.

She had been willing Marquis Evans to ask her on a date for months, yet he consistently—inexplicably—hadn't done it. Chantel didn't get it. She was hot, a great dancer, and had a huge social media following. Guys were lining up to date her, though she hadn't found any guy who checked the boxes like Marquis. Maybe he was intimidated by her?

In some ways, she saw it as a challenge. Eventually she would win him; she always won, just like last night. Stack of cash yesterday, a date with Marquis next. Except now she was kind of mad at him for what he did to her after the competition and wanted to ask him about it. She'd allow him a chance to explain.

She fumbled for her cell phone on the nightstand and slipped it under the covers with her. She dialed his number and waited for him to answer.

***

When Chantel's call came through, Marquis Evans' phone was screen up on their living room coffee table. His father, sitting on the couch reading the morning news, peeked around the paper to see who was calling. Marquis, sitting in the leather chair adjacent the couch, reading on a tablet, launched his body out of the seat in an effort to grab the phone before his dad saw Chantel's name and scandalous (by his family's standards) photo. Mission failed. His father raised his eyebrows and gave his son that look he gave when he disapproved of something. "Chantel? Who's that?"

"A dancer I know," Marquis said. The phone, now in his possession, continued to ring.

"Aren't you going to answer?"

Marquis stared at the ringing phone, wishing it would stop. No way he would take a call from Chantel in front of his dad. The phone rang again.

"She looks, you know, a lot older than you," his dad said.

"She's not," Marquis said.

"I take it you don't like her?"

"No, she's okay." It wasn't that Marquis didn't like Chantel, he did, but . . .

"But she can't dance? . . . "

"Who can't dance?" Mrs. Evans said, walking into the living room wearing riding boots and equestrian pants. She sat on the couch and held out a foot to her husband.

Marquis chuckled as he watched his dad struggle to help his mom remove her boots. His ringing phone had clicked over to voicemail and he waited to see if Chantel would leave a message. His mom asked again who they were talking about. Marquis gave Chantel's name and told them she was a good dancer. She *was* a good dancer, one of the best he knew. He also suspected she liked him, but he didn't really know what to do with that. He looked at his dad dressed in his nice golf attire and his mom in her expensive riding clothes and tried to imagine bringing Chantel over to meet them dressed in her usual attire.

"She's too old for him anyway," his dad said.

His mother asked to see her photo, to which Marquis first objected but then acquiesced because he wasn't trying to hide anything. Chantel was who she was. That was on her. His mother glanced at it and said, "I agree with Dad. Way too old."

Later, he checked his phone for the voicemail, but Chantel hadn't left one. He knew what she was calling about anyway. He hadn't had a chance to talk to her after the competition and some of the things she had said to him about Casey's dance with Ekandem made him think she might be jealous of her friend. It probably didn't sit well with her that he had intentionally sought out Casey after the competition instead of her.

Curious about Casey, Marquis pulled up her Instagram account. He watched two videos from last night, one at the club and one at her home before she went out. He hadn't realized it last night, but Casey was dressed in exactly the same barely-there style Chantel favored. He scrolled backwards through her videos and was surprised at her transformation. She went from being cute and strait-laced with a modest dance style to a shameless, suggestive, steamy Chantel clone. Why would she do that, he wondered. He preferred the original version.

CHAPTER SIX

The morning after the competition, Casey awoke still basking in the excitement of it all. She had to keep pinching herself to be sure it wasn't all a dream. Had she really danced with Ekandem Essiet? Had the amazing choreographer, whose videos she watched all the time, singled her out of the crowd? And had Marquis Evans actually talked to her afterwards? Even told her she had danced good? Yes, yes, and yes!

Still in pajamas, Casey booted up her laptop and pulled up one of Ekandem's YouTube videos. In this one he was dancing with a twenty-something-year old girl, very pretty and a good dancer. Standing at her computer, Casey mimicked the girl's moves. When she couldn't quite get the steps on the first try, she'd rewind and replay, practicing until she got it right. She did this for a while, imagining that she was the girl in the video with Ekandem, until a knock on her bedroom door interrupted her. She quickly closed her laptop, sat down at her desk, and pulled out a textbook. She flipped to a random page and, knowing who it was, said, "Come on in, Mom."

Kelly Henderson entered the room, glancing around the space. "Well at least you're up."

"Two tests on Monday," Casey replied, pretending to be absorbed with reading her assignment.

Her mother walked over to where Casey sat and placed a credit card and handwritten list on the desk.

"Grocery list. Add what you need for yourself," she said.

"Really? Thanks, Mom."

"I said *need*, not stuff you just want. There's a difference." Casey sighed and nodded.

Her mother continued speaking. "Money's tight, Casey. Prices are up... On everything."

"I know, Mom." Casey fiddled with a pencil, tapped the eraser on the textbook.

"Do you? I mean... It's brutal, Casey. We've lost... I don't know how many nurses since the pandemic... These double shifts." Her mother's voice trailed off and Casey detected stress and, maybe, sadness. Being a single mom wasn't easy for her mother. Casey knew this and tried to help out when she could.

Her mother walked over to the picture collage wall that held photos of friends and family. She glanced through each picture as she did sometimes when she came to talk to her daughter but didn't quite know what else to say. Casey had figured out long ago that it was a way for her mother to feel connected and involved in her life. Now that her mom worked so many shifts at the hospital, she and Casey didn't spend as much time together as they once had, and that made both of them sad.

Pausing at one of the photos, Casey's mom studied the image, lost in her thoughts of how things used to be. The 5x7 photo, taken years ago, was a professional portrait of the three of them—Casey, her mother and father. Casey, around three or four years old, sat between her parents, wearing a cute frilly blue with pink flowers dress, a matching bow in her hair, and white lace socks with Mary Jane shoes. Everything was perfect about that photo except when Casey, at the last minute had stuck out her tongue and made a silly face at the camera. Her mother hadn't been happy about the result of that picture, but Casey remembered her dad loving it. That picture brought him so much joy that he kept it hanging on a bulletin board at his office until the day he died. Then someone packed up all his belongings and sent them home in a box, including the picture. Casey claimed it for her own and hung it on her wall.

Even though it had been several years since her dad had died, it sometimes seemed like yesterday. Casey was certain there'd always be a dad-sized hole in her heart.

Her mother sighed and turned away from the wall of memories. "I've got to go," she said, giving Casey a quick kiss on the forehead. Casey felt tears well up. She wanted to comfort her mother but didn't know what to say.

At the door her mother stopped and turned back toward her. "It looks like that coffee shop is still looking for a cashier. Why don't you stop by on the way to the grocery?"

Casey thought about her plan to become a paid influencer, but knew now was not the time to share that with her mother. "Ah, a job . . . Well—"

A blast of music interrupted them as Casey was saved by a phone call. Ringtone and name confirmed it was Chantel. She had yet to talk to her about the competition and wanted to hear all about it from Chantel's perspective. She didn't want to blow off her mom but she wanted to answer the call. She gestured for her mother to wait a second while she answered the call. She could tell Chantel she needed to call her back, which she knew would annoy her friend, but that was a risk she was willing to take for her mom. However, her mom, looking disappointed, shook her head, walked out of the bedroom and shut the door behind her.

Great, now mom's mad at me, she thought. She did her best to shake that downer mood off and sound upbeat as she answered the call. "Hey, girl! I was just thinking about you. I didn't get a chance to congratulate—"

"—no worries. I noticed you were . . . Busy." Chantel's implication was obvious. Casey rolled her eyes, not in the mood to get into the whole Marquis Evans thing.

"Um . . . yeah. So, what's up?" She acted casual, refusing to take Chantel's bait.

"Not much. I'm still in bed, just hanging out. Wanna come over?"

Casey looked at her textbook, picked up the grocery list, considered her options, not sure what to say. When she remained unresponsive for a beat too long for Chantel's liking, her friend quipped, "Got something going with your *new* friend?"

"My new . . .?" Sophia popped into her mind and Casey quickly dismissed it. "No, I'd love to."

"Nobody home. Door's not locked. Just come on up."

"Got it. See ya," Casey said, ending the call. Dread bubbled up. She dropped her head into her hands and wondered why she had agreed to go over. She had homework, grocery shopping, and her mom wanted her to get a job. Ugh! All she wanted to do was watch dance videos and practice her moves. Instead, she started to straighten her desk and bring some order back into her space before heading to Chantel's.

CHAPTER SEVEN

Casey let herself into Chantel's house and walked through the kitchen and living room, following the sound of the music blaring from the back hallway. Chantel's bedroom was on the right. Casey slowly opened the door, knowing that she never knew what might be blocking it on the other side. She stepped into the room and instantly felt her anxiety kick in. She loved Chantel but that girl did not know how to keep her room clean.

Casey stood at the door, looking at the mess that greeted her. Trophies and plaques lined several shelves. Clothes were piled on the floor. The bed was unmade. The trash can nearly overflowed. And Chantel's closet was opened and looked like a monster tornado had spun up and gone to business inside. Clothes were haphazardly hung on mismatched hangers and shoved on the rack wherever Chantel could find room. Her shoes were scattered on the closet floor in no particular order or pairs. Extra bed linens spilled over the top rack. Seeing that mess made Casey's breath shallow.

Chantel danced in front of a floor to ceiling mirror that lined the entire wall. She had, amazingly, cleared a big enough space for dancing. She waved Casey over. "Come on! I'll show you what it takes to win Dance 4 Cash."

Casey smiled, took her backpack off, removed her phone from her jeans pocket and placed it on the nightstand. She took a place behind Chantel and waited for instructions.

Chantel started off by showing her the new choreography she had been working on. The moves were sexy—signature Chantel, with plenty of hip sways, but something about this dance was even more risqué than usual. Casey watched Chantel closely, imitated her the best she could. At first she struggled and felt embarrassed by the suggestive moves. This wasn't Casey's usual style. Several times Chantel looked pleased that Casey couldn't quite get the complex steps right. Casey kept at it, even though it didn't completely align with what she wanted to present to the world, and by the middle of the afternoon, she could do each move well.

After exhausting themselves dancing, the girls decided they were hungry and fixed a frozen pizza. They sat on the floor in Chantel's room and ate. They popped open a couple of sodas and chatted about last night's competition.

"You could be a choreographer," Casey said.

"Me? Get out..." Chantel sounded genuinely taken aback by the comment, which surprised Casey. She knew her friend knew she was an excellent dancer, so it seemed incredulous to Casey that she wouldn't already know she could be a choreographer, that she hadn't considered it or that she had doubts about herself.

"I'm serious. Choreography by Chantel," she said, making a gesture like her words were on a billboard. "You'd be good."

"Enough of that," Chantel said, wiping her mouth with a napkin. "Ready?" She tossed the napkin onto the paper plate with some leftover pizza crust, and pushed the plate out of the way.

"For what?" Casey asked.

Chantel stood up. "You've got the moves down. Let's put it all together for your new routine."

Casey wiped her mouth and put her plate on top of Chantel's. She grabbed her phone off the nightstand to check the time.

"It's after three. I should go. My mother's on my case about getting a job."

"You don't need a job. I can get you an audition with Josh."

"What!?"

"I can. I'm not playing ya. You forget how much money I made last night?"

Casey hadn't forgotten that envelope of cash they handed Chantel. Getting in front of Josh for an audition would be a dream come true, the necessary first step in becoming a contestant in the competition. Could Chantel really pull that off for her? If she could, and Casey was actually selected as one of the dancers... *Oh my god,* she thought. It was exactly what needed to happen to grow her social media platform.

Against her better judgment, she set her phone back down, pushed her mother's grocery list and job search out of her mind, and made her decision. She stayed and worked extra hard to get the dance routine perfected.

Drained of energy, the girls both collapsed onto the floor, laughing and enjoying the joy they felt from all the dancing. They sat with their backs against the mirror and chatted. Eventually Chantel stood up to grab them both a water from the mini-fridge in the corner of her room, but as she headed there, Casey's phone, still on the nightstand, rang.

Instantly Casey thought, *Oh crap,* the happiness draining from her body as she remembered the grocery list. "If that's my mother, I'm in big trouble," she said.

The phone continued to ring so Chantel grabbed it off the nightstand to toss to Casey, but as she flipped the phone over she stopped and stared at the screen.

Casey didn't think much of it at the time. "Let it ring," she told her.

Without acknowledging Casey, Chantel placed the phone back on the stand and grabbed a bottle of water from the fridge. Casey asked who was on the phone.

Coolly she said, "You got lucky. It wasn't your mother." She turned and stared straight at Casey, unhappy about something.

"What?" Casey asked, confused as to the sudden attitude change.

"Last night, when they gave me the money, everyone was all around me, remember that?"

Casey nodded but she didn't know what that had to do with the phone call. She thought back to the previous night and remembered how she had planned to congratulate Chantel but when everyone had swarmed her at the end, she and Sophia decided to leave because it was late, and then—oof, it hit her. The tap on the shoulder. The surprise when she turned around to find Marquis Evans there.

"What were you and Maquis talking about anyway?"

Casey shifted uncomfortably, pulled her legs in to sit crossed legged. "Just talking, you know?" She sounded more defensive than she had meant to. Marquis had ended up walking her and Sophia out of the dance club. They had chatted about the competition. He had complimented her on the dance with Ekandem. She had told him how good he did and how she thought he should have won, not that she would ever confess that to Chantel.

"About?" Chantel prodded, taking a swig of water, squeezing the bottle tight enough to make the plastic crackle.

Casey tried to figure out what the real issue was. Obviously Chantel was upset Marquis had talked to Casey, but why was that such a big deal? Sure she thought Marquis was good looking, but she doubted they'd ever talk again. He was just being nice to her last night. Though she found Chantel's line of questioning to be somewhat antagonistic, she proceeded carefully. "Why do you want to know?"

"Cause I'm wondering why he just called you."

He just called me? Casey's mind screamed, though she tried to play it cool and not give anything away. Marquis Evans called her? How'd he even get her number? Sophia possibly. Though giddy on the inside, she set her face and calmed her emotions on the outside. "It was nothing, okay?" She stood up and started to gather her things, grabbed her backpack as her mind raced. "And how am I supposed to know why he called?" She reached for her phone that was back on the nightstand, but Chantel was quicker and snatched it up. Casey huffed, held out her hand, and gave Chantel a look that said not a cool thing to do. "Give it to me," she demanded.

Chantel smiled deviously and said, "Let's see if he left you a message."

A Better Way

The last thing Casey wanted was Chantel checking her messages. It would be a total violation of her privacy. She snatched her phone away and stuffed it into her pocket before Chantel could grab it again. "This is crazy!" she said and stormed out of the room and headed for home.

CHAPTER

EIGHT

On the walk home Casey texted and invited Sophia over. She needed someone to confide in about everything that had happened. Before Sophia arrived, Casey had spent time cleaning her room. She had been stuck in Chantel's mess all day so being back in her own organized room was a relief. When Sophia arrived they sat on the bed and Casey recalled the entire day of dancing and how fun it had been all the way up until Marquis called.

"I'm serious, Sophia. She wanted to know if he left a voicemail. And she expected me to let her listen to it! Can you believe that?"

"What did you do?"

"I grabbed my phone and ran out."

Sophia nodded her approval. "You did the right thing. She's just jealous."

Casey knew this was probably true. She had thought about it the entire walk home and had come to the same conclusion. Chantel wasn't used to competition, not that Casey wanted to be her competition, but last night was kind of a big deal. Showing up in her super-hot outfit, getting to dance with Ekandem, talking to Marquis . . . Casey had leveled up last night. She was on the verge of a breakthrough, and she had the likes on her video to prove it. She was sure Chantel had seen her latest video posted, the one Sophia took of her dance with Ekandem. Chantel also knew Casey wasn't as good of a dancer as she was, so if it wasn't the dancing that tipped the jealousy scale, it must have been Marquis.

"But I didn't do anything wrong, Sophia." Casey pleaded her case. It wasn't her fault Marquis had called. She hadn't asked him to, though, if she were being honest, she was thrilled that he had.

Sophia validated her reasoning. She also didn't think Casey had done anything wrong, but was curious. "So did he? Leave a message?"

A playful grin spread across Casey's lips as her whole face lit up.

"What did he say?" Sophia asked excitedly.

"I haven't listened to it yet."

Sophia's mouth dropped open. "No way. You're kidding, right?"

Casey shrugged. "I don't want to know. I mean, I do, but I'm scared."

"No, you're weird. You have to listen, Casey!"

"What if he asks me out? What then?" Of course there was a part of her that absolutely wanted him to, but she also didn't want Chantel to be even more upset with her. She wasn't even sure why Chantel was making it such a big deal. It wasn't like Chantel was dating him, though she had declared him off limits to everyone else. That wasn't fair in Casey's opinion, not if the guy didn't want to go out with her anyway.

"You say yes," Sophia said, responding to Casey's dilemma.

"But Chantel. What about her?"

Sophia picked up Casey's cell phone and handed it to her, basically giving her no choice in the matter. "Play the voicemail. I'll hold your hand if you want." She gave a cheeky smile and offered her hand.

Casey declined the hand but silently gave herself a pep talk. She was seventeen, after all, old enough to play it cool around guys. She told herself that he was just some boy who called her. No big deal.

"Okay, here goes." Casey pulled up his message, clicked the play arrow, and hit speaker.

"Hey, Casey. This is Marquis."

Casey's stomach did a flip flop when she heard his voice. She pushed pause, bit her thumb, unable to continue listening.

"What are you doing?" Sophia asked.

Too many what ifs swirled around Casey's mind. "I can't listen. What about Chantel?" Her mind stacked up the only two possibilities for his call. He really was calling to ask her out or he wasn't calling to ask her out. No matter what else he said those were the only two possibilities, and either one had consequences. She would be thrilled if he asked her out, but then she'd have to deal with Chantel. Or, if he wasn't calling to ask her out, she'd have to deal with the rejection. "Maybe I should delete it. If he really wants to ask me out, he'll call back. Right?"

"What are you, twelve years old? Finish it!"

Casey's heart pounded in her chest. Her nerves were getting the best of her. Sophia was right. She should get it over with and listen, then she'd know. She hit play and Marquis's sexy voice started again.

"We met last night and . . . Um . . . Anyway, can you give me a call? You know, whenever. Thanks."

The two girls looked at each other, both stunned by the message, not sure what to say.

A hard knock on Casey's bedroom door startled both of them. Before Casey had a chance to say come in her mother barged in. By the look on her face, Casey knew she was in a bad mood. Sophia must have sensed that too because she immediately hopped off the bed and started gathering her things.

"Mom! What are you doing?"

Standing her ground at the door, her mother glowered at them. Sophia quickly zipped up her bag and gave Casey a wide-eyed "uh oh" look coupled with a small wave as she headed to the door. She greeted Casey's mom and said, "I'm Sophia and I'm leaving."

Stone-faced, Casey's mom nodded slightly and stepped aside so Sophia could make her escape. Both Casey and her

A Better Way

mom waited until they heard the front door open and close before saying anything.

Casey spoke first. "You're home, *now*? What happened?"

Casey's mom laid into her. "I'm so disappointed in you, Casey. I hardly know you anymore. Last night, you went out looking like a street-walker. What did you do today?"

Casey bristled at being called a prostitute. It wasn't like she was out trying to pick up a bunch of random guys. She was just trying to create an image that helped her social media platform. Her mom wouldn't understand so no point in trying to explain. "Today, I went over to Chantel's." She remembered then that she had meant to stop by the grocery on her way home but had been sidetracked by Marquis's call. Guilt pooled in her chest. "I lost track of time, Mom. I'm sorry."

"Can't eat sorry, young lady, " her mom said sarcastically. "My credit card? . . . You do still have it?"

Casey hopped off the bed and retrieved the credit card from the same spot her mother had placed it earlier. She realized that wasn't a good look. Even if she had stopped at the grocery on her way home from Chantel's she wouldn't have been able to buy any food. Her mind had been on other things and she had completely forgotten to grab it on her way out. She handed it to her mom, who took it and flashed her a disapproving look.

"I was hoping that you would have at least had it in your pocket or your backpack."

"Mom, I'm really sorry."

Her mom shook off the apology. "I won't waste time asking about the job. I'm beat. I came home hungry. . . So much for that. I'm going to bed."

"But why are you home early? You said you had a second shift."

Her mother's posture slumped slightly. "They said I should go home."

"Why?"

She hugged her arms into her body, holding each elbow. "I lost a patient today. She was your age. Reminded me of you."

Casey could see the sadness on her mother's face. "Covid?"

"Yeah, a new variant. She was very sick. We put her on a ventilator right away. In fact, just one week ago today. This afternoon, I was holding her hand when she passed."

The gravity of what her mother had been through hit Casey hard at that moment. Her mother worked hard every day and dealt with incredibly stressful and sad situations. Casey couldn't imagine what it felt like to be with someone when they passed. She hadn't been allowed in the hospital room when her dad had been sick. She had been too young. Her mom had been there for his passing though. Casey felt her heart swell for her mom. She had asked Casey to do two things, go to the grocery and find a job, and Casey had blown it. "Mom . . ." She bowed her head trying to find the right words but couldn't get them to come out of her mouth. Tears threatened her eyes, but Casey fought them back.

Her mom said, "You really messed up today, Casey. It can't happen again, and only you can fix it." With that advice, her mother left her bedroom, leaving Casey all alone to think about everything crushing in on her emotions.

CHAPTER

NINE

The next day, Casey woke up feeling grieved over everything: her mother's disappointment, Chantel's demands, Marquis's vague message, her stagnate social media platform. She had hoped a good night's sleep would alleviate some of her suffering, but when she woke up still bummed out, she decided to hide in her room for some alone time. She thought about posting a confessional video to her account asking for advice but decided against that. Even though her followers would love it, Chantel wouldn't and her mom would be upset that she was messing around online rather than looking for a job.

She decided to get dressed, hoping it would motivate her to practice dancing, but, instead, found herself scrolling through Marquis's TikTok account. He had a mixture of serious dance videos where he showed off his moves, and funny videos where he performed these hysterical skits about things that had happened in his life. Casey watched the one where he did a comical routine on what it was like to lose a dance contest. Casey busted out laughing. Not only was he a talented dancer, but he was really funny. She loved that combo. She pushed replay for the fourth time but paused it when a text notification from Sophia popped up on her phone.

Sophia: hey casey. have you looked at chantel's tiktok page today

Casey: no do I have to
Sophia: only if you care about ur reputation
Bolting upright in bed, **Casey** texted: hold on, Im calling

Casey bounded off the bed, rushed to her desk, and opened her laptop. She told Siri to call Sophia, who picked up on first ring.

"Where are you?" Casey asked.

"I'm at the mall. I'm sitting outside."

Good, Casey thought. She didn't want anyone eavesdropping on the conversation. "Okay. I'm on her account."

"Good. Tell me that's not you she's talking about."

Casey watched the video Chantel had posted earlier that morning, her heart pounding at what she heard. Chantel appeared on camera, wearing full makeup and hair styled. Casey scrutinized her every word:

> "Bestie. Everybody has one. Right? Maybe, if you're real lucky, you got more than one. So, tell me this. What do you do when someone, who's *supposed* to be your Bestie, is making a play for your guy, not even behind your back, but right there while you're watching him."

Casey felt the heat rise to her cheeks, a mash of emotions brewing under her skin. Chantel was most definitely talking about her. Casey dreaded reading the comments but there were already so many. She glanced through the first few:

> **Keisha Greene**: How do you know she wasn't just talking? Maybe she wasn't moving on him?
> **Chantel Jackson**: The why did he call her?
> **Darlene Bouey**: Did you ask her?
> **Chantel Jackson**: She said it was nothing.
> **Darlene Bouey**: Course she did. Girl, that's proof it was something.

Brandon Jones: Hey, Chantel, Face it, you've got yourself one nasty Bestie. :(
Chantel Jackson: Got that right.
Brandon Jones: Call her out, Chantel. Everybody who knows you already knows who you're talking about.

Casey groaned and set her phone aside. She clicked out of TikTok and dropped her head into her hands. She couldn't believe this was happening.

Sophia, still on the other end of the abandoned phone call, shouted Casey's name a couple times. "Are you there?"

Casey picked up the phone and said, "Yeah, I'm here. Tell me. Did she?" She bit her lip, terrified by what the response would be.

"No! That one girl, Keisha, talked her out of it."

"Good." Casey breathed a sigh of relief, wanting to believe that her identity wouldn't be blasted all over the Internet, but Sophia reminded her what that guy named Brandon had said.

"He's right, Casey. Most people know. What are you going to do?"

She thought about this for a moment before saying, "I don't know." That was the truth. She didn't know what she was going to do. All she did know was her stomach felt queasy and she had the urge to clean and organize desk drawers.

She told Sophia she had to go and hung up the phone. But instead of cleaning, she turned off the lights, crawled back into bed, and pulled the covers over her head.

CHAPTER TEN

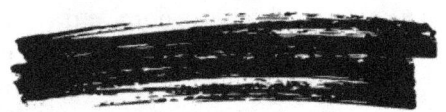

Casey wasn't sure how long she had been in bed crying when the knock on the door came. She must have alternated between crying and dozing off for a couple of hours. The knock startled her out of a light troubled sleep, but she didn't answer.

She heard the door creak open and her mother's voice: "Casey?"

When Casey didn't respond, her mother flipped on the light. "What are you doing?"

Casey, still under the covers, could sense movement around her bed, then the sound of her blinds being pulled open, allowing sunshine to stream in.

"Are you sick?" her mother asked.

Casey pulled the cover off her face so her mother could see she was still alive. "Not sick, mom."

Her mother sat on the edge of the bed and looked at her daughter's face. Casey knew her eyes must be puffy and red from all the crying.

"What's wrong then?" She tenderly laid a hand against Casey's forehead to check for fever.

Casey frowned and scooted out from under the sheets. She was fully dressed, even in shoes, which was something she never allowed on her bed. That's how upset she had been after the earlier Chantel debacle. She pushed herself off the bed, needing to go to the bathroom. She saw the concerned look on her mom's face and felt bad for making her mom

A Better Way

worry. "I just had a bad day," she said, trying to make it sound like no big deal.

She walked into the bathroom that connected to her room and the hallway and shut the door. From inside the bathroom, she talked to her mom through the door. "Haven't you ever had a bad day? You know, when you just want to be alone, in the dark?"

"Lately, it's been hard to find a good day," her mom responded.

Casey finished up in the bathroom and returned to her bedroom. Her mom held up a glossy flyer. "This was in today's mail. It's from school. Addressed to me, I guess . . ." She read the address off the label: "To the parents of Casey Henderson."

That assumption, that there were two parents in the household, still pained her mom. It was an unwelcomed reminder of what—who—was missing from their home.

Casey wasn't that interested in the mailer. She was more interested in finding her phone at the moment. She searched the bed covers, looked under the pillows, patted and scrunched the sheets a few times but no phone. "Where is it?" she said under her breath, her irritation rising.

Her mother held up the mailer. "Do you know what this is about?"

Casey rummaged around the bed one more time and finally came up with the prize. "There you are," she said, relieved. She glanced at her mother and saw furrowed brows and a pinched mouth. If she wasn't careful she would annoy her mother to the point of being grounded. She stepped in closer to get a look at the flyer and shrugged. "A scholarship I hope?"

"Were you expecting a call?" Her mother asked flippantly.

"Not really . . . So, what is it?" She gestured to the piece of mail her mother held.

Kelly pressed her lips into a thin line. "Have you ever heard of Marc Mero?"

"Marc? . . . TikTok?" She said, trying to jog her memory of the name. She might have seen his name somewhere.

"Instagram, right?" Truth was she had no idea who Marc Mero was or why her mother was asking about him.

"It says here he's an American former amateur boxer and professional wrestler, and a motivational speaker." She watched her daughter's face for any recognition but Casey shrugged. Her mother added, "He made a presentation at school."

"Oh him!" Casey remembered him now. "It was an optional assembly, Mom. I didn't go, but I heard some of the kids talking about it."

Kelly feigned surprise. "You had a chance to skip class and be excused, but you didn't?"

"I had an AP test right after. I was studying. Come on, Mom. I think I made the right decision. I got an A by the way."

Kelly handed the flyer to Casey. "Here. Your guidance department sent this out for any students who would like to meet with him one on one. It's free."

"Mom, I didn't go. Why would I need to see him? The kids said he was cool, but it's for the kids who are messed up."

Her mother gave her a look that said *and what are you?* Casey knew her mother was worried about her and was upset about some of the things she had or hadn't done recently, but this was ridiculous. "I'm fine," she insisted. "Okay?"

"Just read it over. Promise me you will. Casey?"

Arguing with her mother would be futile so she nodded and promised.

Her mother smiled, looked satisfied. "I've got the midnight shift tonight. I'm going to get some sleep." She kissed her daughter on the cheek and walked out of the room.

Since she didn't want to break a promise to her mother, Casey glanced over the flyer, not particularly interested in reading it thoroughly. She figured looking it over made good on her word, so, when she finished, she dropped it into the wastebasket.

CHAPTER

ELEVEN

The early morning sun filtered through Casey's bedroom blinds. Casey, sprawled out on her desk, used a textbook as a pillow. The soft whir of the air conditioning lulled her in and out of a restless sleep. She was dreaming about being stuck to an old wooden school chair and handed a stack of exams by someone dressed as a giant turkey. She tried frantically to work her way through the exams in the allotted time but the pile kept growing larger and larger. Just as the pile was about to tip over, Casey's phone rang, startling her awake. In her confusion to silence the device, and shake away the terrifying dream, she accidentally knocked the phone off the edge of the desk where it landed in the wastebasket. It rang again, as if wailing to be saved from its predicament.

The grogginess lingered in her head as she tried to reach for it around the side of her desk but couldn't quite get it. She rolled the stiffness out of her neck as she scooted closer, needing to stand and lean over her desk to grab it. As her fingers closed around the still ringing phone, she noticed the flyer she had thrown away yesterday. She made a note to conceal it under other discarded paper so her mother wouldn't see it if she happened to look. But that task would have to wait until she answered the FaceTime call from Sophia.

"Hey," Casey said when the call connected. "I was asleep. I mean I guess I fell asleep here. Studying..."

"It's Saturday morning, Casey. Why would you—"
"It's what I do . . . Sometimes anyway. So this isn't more about Chantel, is it?"
"No, well, not exactly."
Casey groaned. "I don't do *not exactly*."
"Here's the thing, I've been thinking, she's turned against you, right? Why?"
"You know why. Marquis."
"Not exactly."
Ugh, there was that phrase again. She flashed Sophia an annoyed look.
"Let me finish," Sophia said. "What I mean is that he's only part of it. You're a threat to her. Not just to move in on Marquis."
"I didn't move on him and you know it!"
"Chill. Of course I do. But hear me out. She's afraid you are also a better dancer."
Casey balked at that idea. No one was better than Chantel. She had the followers and the Dance 4 Cash winnings to prove it. "Get out, Sophia. Me?"
"Maybe not right now, but she knows you can be . . . Soon. That's why she's lying and making you look like you're the bad guy. She wants you to give up so she can have it all."
Casey thought about this for a moment. It had never occurred to her that she could be a better dancer than Chantel. But what Sophia said kind of made sense. The way Chantel seemed to get satisfaction the other day when Casey couldn't perfect each dance move she had choreographed. Also, it had been bothering Casey that Chantel was pushing her to dress a certain way, risqué beyond her comfort zone. At first she had thought her *bestie* was just trying to help her, but now she wondered if there had been an ulterior motive all along.
"And what can I do about it?" Casey asked.
"You can't play her game. That's for sure. It's not who you are. It would be fake. And you can't live your life based on what other people think of you. You have to believe in yourself, Casey."

A Better Way

Casey felt tears sting her eyes as she stared at the ever-present bible on her desk. It had been weeks since she opened it. Her bottom lip trembled.

Sophia noticed and said, "Stop that. Feeling sorry for yourself isn't the answer. I'm coming over. I've got an idea. Oh, and get dressed!"

CHAPTER

TWELVE

To execute Sophia's idea, the girls had driven thirty minutes across town and were now sitting in Sophia's car in the parking lot of a busy strip-mall with a variety of businesses, including a pizza joint, a Chinese restaurant, a dentist office, a nail salon, and an urgent care. But the girls weren't interested in any of those places; Their attention focused on the business with a giant purple poster in the window that said "Come Dance with Us Today!" This wasn't just any dance studio. This one belonged to Ekandem Essiet and was considered the premiere dance studio of Orlando. Casey had tried to get into classes here before but they were always booked. She was stunned her friend was able to get them a spot. Sophia had told her on the drive over how she had seen an ad for a dance Master Class on TikTok. She knew how much Casey admired Ekandem and how upset she had been about the Chantel issue. She booked it as a surprise and pick-me-up.

The girls lingered in the car, watching as dancers dressed in a variety of styles started to head inside the studio. Casey's nerves flared up.

"What if Chantel is here?"

"She won't be," Sophia said, sounding much surer about that than Casey felt.

"She better not be," Casey said.

"Classes like this are beneath someone like her. Seriously, Casey. Forget Chantel. Believe in yourself."

A Better Way

Casey and Sophia entered the studio to find it packed with wall-to-wall dancers, male and female, ranging in age from ten to twenty-five. The loud music and nervous energy filled the wide-open space. Floor to ceiling windows formed one wall overlooking the parking lot while full length mirrors covered the opposite wall. Dancers milled about, chatting, stretching, warming up.

The girls slipped in unnoticed and settled into their own tiny spot amongst the dancers. Casey felt overwhelmed by the amount of people who had shown up for the Master Class. She leaned over close to Sophia's ear, cupped her hand to block out the noise, and said, "Can't get much done with this many dancers." Sophia nodded in agreement.

The crowd suddenly quieted down as a door off to the side of the studio opened and Ekandem stepped out. An instant ovation rocked the studio as the students clapped and whistled. Somewhere, someone lowered the music. A spotlight flicked on, centering on Ekandem as he danced his way to a taped X on the floor.

"Beyond amazing!" he said, acknowledging the turn out. "Thanks to all of you for coming out this morning. Don't be discouraged by the size of this class. I have two assistants with me today. We'll break you out into groups later to make sure you get all the attention you'll need."

Casey and Sophia smiled at each other, both excited for the breakout groups.

The music cranked up louder and Ekandem started to dance. Everyone took a seat on the hardwood floor and watched, mesmerized, as he moved in perfect rhythm to the beats around the lacquered hardwood floor. His moves amazing. His footwork precise. He ran through an entire routine and when he finished, the crowd broke out into a raucous applause. He then started over, this time explaining his choreography, offering instructions on how to make each move perfect.

He paused and said, "See, Simple stuff. Right?" Everyone laughed. "Hang in there. It gets easier. Seriously, it does."

He motioned toward the same side door he had entered from. "Meet my partners for this routine and my assistants who will work with you later." The door opened and two people emerged. "Marquis and Chantel," Ekandem said, as the two of them started to dance into the studio.

Casey gasped and froze. The shock and anger instantly welled in her body. Still seated, she grabbed Sophia's arm roughly and turned her so they were facing each other. Sophia looked surprised at the turn of events, too, but Casey already blamed her in her mind.

"You knew! You had to!" Casey yelled. The music had been lowered when Ekandem made the introductions, so Casey's sudden loud shout seized everyone's attention, who all turned to look. Sophia's expression showed panic and embarrassment. "No. I swear! Casey, I had no idea."

All eyes were on them, even Chantel's and Marquis's, who had stopped dancing and now stood gawking at the commotion.

Casey assessed the situation, feeling embarrassment but no remorse at her outburst, she stood up. Quietly to Sophia she said, "I'm out. I can't believe you did this."

Casey turned to leave but there was no direct path to the door. She started to step around the many seated dancers. As she weaved her way through the crowd, all she wanted to do was shove open the exit door and make her escape. But Chantel's voice stopped her in her tracks. "Take a good look, everybody. This is Casey who obviously came here today to ruin everything. When you have no talent, and don't even look like a dancer, I guess this is what you do. Right, Casey?"

Chantel stomped across the studio, her look full of contempt. The girls stood face to face now. Tears pricked Casey's eyes as she stared speechless at the girl who used to be her best friend.

All eyes trained on them, no one made a sound. Casey glanced over at Marquis who looked on in disbelief at the unfolding scene. Casey wanted to disappear. Chantel sneered and continued her rant. "I tried to help you once, didn't I? Showed you what to wear. Even gave you some of my sexiest moves. But with that body, there's only so much you can do." Chantel laughed at her own joke. Some of the other dancers picked up on it and laughed too.

Mortified at the insults, Casey's ears burned. She bypassed Chantel and resumed her push toward the exit, trying not to step on anyone or trip and fall. Sophia caught up to her and grabbed her arm, but Casey wrenched it away and gave her a hateful look.

"See," Chantel said. "That's why she has no friends."

Ekandem and Marquis stepped in and told Chantel to stop, but she was relentless in her verbal attack on Casey. As Casey continued toward the exit, Chantel circumvented their efforts to quiet her and rushed to block Casey's way out.

The two girls who used to be best friends stared at each other. Casey couldn't stop crying. Chantel looked like she hated her. "Who's Marquis with now, Casey?" She taunted her, loud enough for people to hear. "Not you, Loser." Smugness filled Chantel's face.

Casey glanced over at Marquis before she pushed her way past Chantel and out the door, but he had his head bowed, not looking at her.

CHAPTER

THIRTEEN

The Uber pulled up to the curb outside her house and Casey slid out of the backseat. She mumbled a thanks to the driver and rushed inside. She didn't want her nosy next door neighbor to see her and think something was wrong and feel the need to check on her. She was a wreck, though, and didn't bother to close the front door after she plowed through it. She had cried all the way home, ignored the frantic texts from Sophia, and let several calls from Marquis go to voicemail. She didn't want to talk to anyone.

She ran upstairs to her bedroom as another text and phone call came through. She powered off her phone and tossed it onto her bed where it took a bounce into the wall.

A mixture of chaotic emotions coursed through her body. Anxiety, anger, distress. She wandered around her room scanning everything, looking for something to tidy up, to help calm her, but her room was already neat and organized. This frustrated her. She eyed her bed and, without knowing what she planned to do until she did it, she reached out and rumpled the comforter. That felt good to her so she rumpled it more. Then in a fit of anger she yanked the covers off the bed onto the floor, pillows scattering in different directions, and stomped on her beautiful floral bedding.

She kept hearing Chantel's voice and seeing all those dancers staring at her. She thought about Sophia and what she had done. She thought they were friends. Casey's jaw clenched like she was biting down on a piece of cardboard and her breathing came hard and fast, like she had just finished an intense workout. The fury in her chest grew as her eyes landed on the Jesus portrait. Her body trembled as she forced herself to look away. She lunged at her desk, screaming her frustrations as she raked her arm across the desk top. In one mighty swoop, she knocked everything onto the floor, her textbooks, bible, lamp, laptop, notepad, pencil cup . . . It all flew off the desk, landing with a crash.

Next Casey turned to the wall of dance posters. With both hands like cat claws, in a frenzy of speed, Casey ripped them all down. They lay in a crumpled pile by her feet.

Casey stopped and stared at the door leading to the bathroom she shared with her mother. An idea, or more like a curiosity took hold of her as she marched into the bathroom and stared at her reflection in the medicine cabinet mirror. She couldn't believe what she saw. Her face was swollen and blotchy. Her nose was red and irritated. Her eyes puffy. She looked like she had been stung by a wasp. And honestly, she had been. Chantel had stung her over and over and over again with her words.

How would she ever be able to face any of those dancers again after they had witnessed Chantel's insults?

She opened the medicine cabinet and took stock of the three shelves: a bottle of Aspirin, a box of Band-Aids, tweezers, a sleeping mask, nasal spray, eye shadow, ear plugs, and a large jar of MiraLAX.

Casey nudged the MiraLAX to the side, revealing behind it a prescription pill bottle. She stared at it for a moment, considering her options, until her curiosity got the better of her. She grabbed the bottle off the shelf and shut the cabinet. The label read:

Kelly Henderson, Diazepam (Valium) 10mg, 30 tablets — no refills.

Casey clutched the pill bottle in her hand and stared at her image. She remembered her mother's words from the other night, when she confessed that she hardly recognized Casey anymore. Staring at herself in the mirror now helped her understand what her mother had meant. Casey didn't recognize herself either. Who was this person holding a bottle of pills, staring back at her. Was she so desperate for attention that she would compromise her own values just to achieve it? Wearing tight, revealing clothes wasn't her thing and, yet, no one had forced her to post a video or go out to the club barely clothed. She had chosen to do that. Why? Because Chantel had insisted that the less she wore the more attention she'd get? Because she needed that kind of attention? She had been brought up to respect her body, not make a spectacle of it. And even though posting things on social media was fun, it had started to rule her life. She had started to crave the dopamine hits that came from the likes as well as the hate. That was hard to admit, but the drama was every bit addictive as it was upsetting.

She stared harder at her image, looked deep into her own eyes, searching for where she had taken the wrong turn.

A voice called her name from downstairs, startling her out of her thoughts. She walked into her bedroom, set the bottle of pills on her desk, and surveyed the mess.

"Casey?" the voice called from the stairway. "Are you up there?"

Casey didn't answer. She was shocked by the state of her room. She knew she had been the one to cause the mess, but she had never experienced wrath like that and was shocked at how it took control over her actions. *This must be what was meant by "blinded by anger,"* she thought.

A knock on her door snapped her out of her thoughts. Sophia's voice through the door: "Casey, Can we talk, please?"

Casey didn't answer.

"Casey, come on."

"I've got nothing to say," she said. Why would she want to talk to the traitor who had set her up in the first place.

"Marquis is here with me," Sophia said.

Casey rolled her eyes. *Of course*, she thought sarcastically, *of course he'd be here to witness this too.* She looked around her wrecked room, feeling defeated.

Sophia was still talking through the door. "Do you remember the night in your room when we were leaving for Dance 4 Cash? After you posted on TikTok, you told your followers you were going to a contest with your new good friend. Remember?"

Casey remained silent.

"Do you know why I asked if you meant it?"

Annoyed with the line of questioning, Casey snarked, "No idea."

"Because after two months of being the new kid at school, not one kid ever looked my way much less said hi . . . Except you."

Casey processed this information. She remembered the day she had met Sophia in fourth period and how grateful Sophia had seemed that someone had finally talked to her. Casey moved closer to the door.

Sophia continued. "That meant everything to me, because I could tell you meant it. Even though you had a lot of friends, you were open enough to include me."

Casey reached the door and placed a hand on it, not sure if she was holding it shut or planning to open it. "Then why would you set me up like you did this morning. How could—"

Marquis interrupted. "Casey, that's her point! Being your friend is too important to her. Why would she risk losing her only friend?"

Casey bowed her head as the truth hit her. She had gotten it all wrong. "God forgive me," she said, quickly opening and shutting the door as she stepped out into the hallway. No way she would let either of them see her bedroom in its current state.

Casey gave Sophia a warm hug. When the two girls separated from the embrace, Casey told her she was sorry. Sophia smiled understandingly and gave Casey another hug.

Now that they knew Casey was okay, Sophia offered to run Marquis home and then come back to hang out. Casey had something she wanted to do though—the pill bottle flashed through her mind—and needed to do it alone. She told Sophia they could hang out another time.

As Sophia and Marquis started down the stairs, Casey realized she still didn't know why Marquis had left that vague voicemail the other day, the one that had started the fight between her and Chantel. She decided to ask him about it.

"Oh, right," Marquis replied, smiling sheepishly. "I just wanted to know if it was okay if someday I could invite you to a Young Life meeting." He cleared his throat. "My parents, they sponsor . . .and maybe we could do dinner . . ."

Her stomach flip-flopped and her mind squealed. *So he was calling to ask me out!* She smiled and casually said, "Dinner? Sure, I'd like that."

Marquis flashed his charming smile and waved goodbye. Casey's spirits lifted as she watched Sophia and Marquis leave her house.

CHAPTER FOURTEEN

A scream roused Casey from a deep slumber. She opened her eyes to darkness. She blinked but couldn't see anything. Vaguely, a voice penetrated her hearing, but it was muffled, like someone was talking through piles of fabric. In her half-asleep state, she couldn't tell what the voice said. *Dreaming*, she told herself, *go back to sleep*. She closed her eyes and tried to sink back into a pleasant sleep. Soon a blast of cool air hit her skin and jarred her alert as the bed covers were peeled back. Again, she opened her eyes, blinked, but was met with pure darkness. Why couldn't she see? Somebody shook her shoulder, gently at first but becoming more frantic. She heard the muted sound of her name being called.

Casey's hand went instinctively to her face, landing on the silk eye mask that covered her eyes. Right! That's why she couldn't see. She pushed it up and blinked as an unexpected bright light hit her retinas. She remembered the earplugs and removed them from each ear. She sat up and tried to orientate herself to the situation.

Her mother, dressed in hospital scrubs, paced while speaking to someone on the phone. She held the now-empty pill bottle in her hand. When she saw Casey sit up in bed, her eyes widened and she told the person on the phone to hold on.

"Casey, did you take this whole bottle of Valium? Did you? How many? Answer me!"

Casey was taken aback by her mother's flustered state. "None, mom! None."

Her mother let out a huge breath and spoke into the phone, apologized, said there was no emergency, and hung up.

She stared at her daughter, waiting for an explanation. Casey explained how she had been exhausted yesterday and had decided to go to bed early. She had seen the mask and ear plugs in the medicine cabinet and since it was still light out she had decided to use them to help her fall asleep. Her mother wanted to know about the pills, so Casey told her how she had flushed the whole bottle down the toilet before she crawled into bed.

Though her mother looked like she believed her, she still exhibited concern. Her brows knitted, she said, "Tell me what's going on. Why did you take them from the cabinet? You were going to take them, weren't you? I need answers, Casey." Her mother looked around at the mess that Casey hadn't bothered to clean up yet and added, "And this room?"

Casey took a deep breath. She decided honesty was the way to go. "Yes, I thought about it. I'm sorry. I have some bad stuff going on, Mom." She hugged her legs into her chest and rested her chin on her knees. She had been so emotionally drained after yesterday's drama that she hadn't had the energy to clean the mess she had made of her room.

"Where is that flyer from the guy who came to school?"

Casey got off the bed, stepped over all the stuff she had dumped off her desk, and reached into the wastebasket. She pulled out the flyer and handed it to her mother.

"I'm calling him right now," Kelly said. "We—you and me—are going to see him."

"Mom—" Casey started to protest but her mother cut her off.

"I'm not asking you. Got it?" She dialed the number and waited for someone to pick up. Part of Casey wanted no one to answer. This whole idea of talking to some stranger made her feel weird. But there was another part of her that wanted help in understanding what was happening to her. Her fate was decided when someone picked up and said hello.

CHAPTER

FIFTEEN

Casey and her mother sat together on a sofa in Marc Mero's office, a standard but plain room. Wall decorations consisted of posters promoting Marc's anti-bullying programs, and substance abuse and suicide prevention messages. There were a few framed photos of him presenting at various schools. The most interesting photo to Casey was the one where Marc was posing in a wrestling ring, dressed only in red and white trunks and matching fringed wrist cuffs with a WWF Championship Belt draped over his shoulder.

On her mother's urging, Casey shared her problems from the last few weeks. At first she hesitated to share anything with this man, but warmed up to him because he seemed to listen and care. Maybe he could help her with Chantel and all the drama after all.

After she finished speaking, Marc Mero, who sat across from them in a leather chair, said, "Casey, pouring your heart out to someone you've never met is tough. It takes guts. I'm proud of you. But now I know what you've been going through. We have a starting point."

"I had no idea," Kelly Henderson said.

Mrs. Henderson . . . Sorry, you said, Kelly. Kelly, most of the time especially at school assemblies, I target the bullies and try to inspire their friends and classmates to stop the bullying instead of ignoring it. We are losing too many students to suicide, drugs, gangs, and violence."

"But what about the victims of bullies?" Kelly asked.

Marc Mero pointed to the "Champion of Choices" banner hanging on the wall behind them.

"I've dedicated my life to helping others be the "Champion" they're destined to be. It's just as true for those who have suffered at the hands of a bully. I know, because I was a victim, too," he said.

He continued sharing his thoughts and background, mentioning the school presentation where he had gone more in depth on his personal story of survival and choice.

Casey shifted in her seat, feeling awkward, like she was being put on the spot. "Sorry," she said. "I opted out of that presentation."

"She had a test," her mother quickly added.

"Well, I did, but I could have gone . . . I just didn't think it was for me. ... Sorry, Mom."

Her mother squeezed her hand.

Marc smiled at the two of them, and said, "That's okay. When you leave here I'll give you a booklet which covers my journey." He sat upright in his chair and clasped his hands together, spoke to both of them: "Sometimes the people you hurt the most are those who love you the most. Mom and daughter may have a little honesty issue to work on."

Casey and Kelly both nodded. Marc went over to the table that held the booklets and other literature. He grabbed one and handed it to Casey.

He told them he was glad they had contacted him and thought they were off to a good start. He asked to see Casey by herself next session. "Make sure you have read that booklet by then, okay?" Casey said she would. "Good. I'm confident that I can show you ways to deal with Chantel, and guide you to become the champion you are destined to be."

He walked them to the front of the office space, and, as they were saying goodbye, Casey noticed the framed quote hanging above the door. "Be yourself. Everyone else is already taken." —Oscar Wilde.

"I like that," Casey said.

"Good. We'll talk about what it can mean for you next time."

CHAPTER

SIXTEEN

After spending a few days cleaning up her room, it was finally back in order: The bed neatly made, not one lump to be seen. The pillows fluffed. The desk tidy, nothing out of place. The lamp, Bible, pencil cup, textbooks and notepad all back in their original spots. In the center, her laptop was opened to a TED Talk video.

Sophia was busy setting up the tripod and phone for recording a video while Casey changed outfits in her closet. At one point, Sophia had yelled through the door to Casey, "Please don't shock Jesus this time." They both cracked up laughing. Sophia had a great sense of humor, which Casey loved about her.

Casey pulled her hair back in a simple ponytail and checked her makeup in the lighted vanity mirror. Ready, she stepped out of the closet.

Sophia swiveled around and checked her out. "Whoa!" she exclaimed, looking shocked, but in a good way. "That's it? I mean, you're going to look like that for this TikTok post?"

"Exactly," Casey said, as she studied her minimalist style choice in front of the floor length mirror. She wore navy blue leggings and a matching sporty long-sleeve cropped T-shirt that exposed only a couple inches of her midriff. She preferred this athleisure vibe than the over-the-top sexy vibe she had experimented with. She still felt sexy in this outfit but not on display. Whereas the club outfit had screamed "Your place or mine," this outfit relayed self-confidence and athleticism. Instead of full makeup with thick liner, lashes and lipstick that made her look like she was in her late twenties, she had opted for a fresh simple look that made her look her age.

"You better introduce yourself all over again, your followers won't know who you are."

They both laughed.

"Wait," Sophia said. "Before we do this . . . What are you going to do about dinner with Marquis?"

Casey thought for a moment, shrugged, and made a funny face. "Eat? I guess?"

"No, I'm serious. Have you ever had *dinner* with rich people before?"

Casey shook her head. "Of course not. Unless sitting next to these people at McDonald's who came in wearing real fur coats once counts. I mean the temp was about sixty-five." In Florida, when the temperature dips below seventy degrees, the locals start putting on their winter clothes. Casey laughed at her own joke.

"Stop. I'm serious." Sophia gave her a look that said she wasn't joking anymore. "Do you want to be embarrassed? Like which fork is for salad?"

Casey thought about it for a moment. She wanted to say whichever one she was using, but she didn't think Sophia would appreciate that joke either, so she kept quiet and shrugged.

Sophia exhaled deeply. "Let's do this video, but, girl, you need help."

***

Marquis sat alone in his living room, with his laptop, watching the TikTok video Casey Henderson had uploaded. Her look was different on this post, dressed down but pulled together. She also wore very little makeup. She looked natural and pretty. Marquis liked this look much better than the over-the-top glam look some girls always wore. Like Chantel. He didn't understand the need to cover up their faces to the point of non-recognition just so they could walk around pretending that was the way they really looked.

He listened as Casey addressed her followers. "Sorry, this isn't easy..." she said, trying to make an excuse for her rambling. Marquis smiled. She seemed so nervous, but he found it charming. He chuckled when she introduced her friend Sophia, who popped her head into the frame from out of nowhere.

A voice behind Marquis, startled him. "Now she's not too old," his mother said.

"Definitely not. And she—"

Marquis flipped around. His parents stood right behind his chair, watching the video. "Mom! Dad! How long have you been there?" He slammed his laptop shut and stood up.

"Long enough. We would love to meet her. Ask her over for dinner. At the club, okay?" His mother said and walked away into another room. Marquis waited a beat or two for his dad to follow but his dad didn't budge.

"Dad?" Marquis said, gesturing, with respect, that maybe his dad could leave too.

His dad grinned. "Sorry, son. But you're here in the living room. What can I say?" But his dad took the suggestion and started to leave the area. Marquis thought of something he wanted to say so he called out to his dad who stopped and turned around.

"She can dance," he said, grinning.

His father nodded and smiled, adding some wise words for Marquis's consideration. "Remember what you believe in." Then Mr. Evans left.

CHAPTER
SEVENTEEN

Sophia, committed to helping Casey get ready for her date with Marquis, had taken it upon herself to research local etiquette classes. Casey didn't understand why she couldn't just Google "how to eat like a rich person" or "fancy ways to hold her knife and fork," to get ready for the date, but Sophia insisted that an in-person class was the only way to elevate her public manners. Sophia found the Master Class advertised on YouTube. However, the only way to sign up was to go in person and meet with the certified etiquette expert named Jackie Vernon Thompson, who would help with registering.

"Have you taken this before?" Casey asked. They were hanging out in her bedroom again.

"No, but I saw a video about her and the Academy. If I ever needed it, I'd go, but the chances of me getting invited to some country club are slim."

Casey shuddered at the thought of going on a date with Marquis's family to a country club. She had never been to a country club so the idea scared her. What if they did have special forks and she chose the wrong one? Or drank from someone else's glass of water by mistake? She liked Marquis and didn't want to embarrass him.

Casey agreed to go register but on certain conditions: Sophia had to drive and go inside with her, and then she had to drive Casey to two other places. Since her mother worked so many double shifts lately, she never had access to their car.

A Better Way

Once Casey told her the two places she needed to go, Sophia agreed.

When the day arrived to register for the etiquette class, Sophia pulled up to the curb and picked Casey up. They had a big day ahead of them with at least three stops planned. The first stop would not be the School of Etiquette, instead, Sophia drove a familiar route, heading toward downtown Orlando.

On the drive they discussed a handful of things. Their friendship was growing and both girls trusted each other. Casey had recently shared with Sophia something Chantel had offered to do for her. It had been offered up on the same day Marquis had called, unknowingly igniting the feud between Casey and Chantel. They had been enjoying their afternoon of dance and Chantel said she would talk to Josh about getting Casey an audition for Dance 4 Cash. Obviously, that wasn't going to happen now that they had the falling out.

When Sophia first heard Casey's plan, she wasn't so sure about it. But as they headed toward the warehouse, she told Casey she was smart for not allowing someone else to control her future.

The warehouse parking lot was empty, except for a red sports car parked next to the building. Casey hoped that meant Josh was inside. She told Casey she'd be right back and stepped out of the car.

The front door was unlocked so Casey walked inside. The space was dim, lit only by a few overhead lights, and whatever sunlight filtered in through the upper windows. Unlike the last time she was there, no crowds were pushing their way in, no leering guys checking her out, no hazy fog tickling her throat. Casey called out a "hello," which echoed off the exposed rafters. No answer. The Dance 4 Cash banner still hung in the same spot but no music pulsed from the speakers. As she roamed around the perimeter, she listened for any sound to guide her direction, but it was eerily quiet. She called out Josh's name. No answer. She continued walking around to the other side of the space where she finally spotted a light coming from an office window. She peeked in and recognized Josh sitting at a desk with headphones on, his back toward her, working on a computer.

She tried knocking several times, but he couldn't hear her. She had come this far so she might as well keep going. She twisted the handle on the door and the door popped open. Casey stepped inside and shouted his name. Startled, he swiveled around and yanked off his headphones.

"You scared the hell out of me!"

She felt terrible and apologized, tried to explain how she knocked—

"Forget it," he said. "What's up?"

Casey took a deep breath. "I don't know if you remember me, I'm—"

"You're Casey. I know. Word gets around."

Casey eyed him suspiciously, feeling herself get defensive. "What does that mean?" The way he said it seemed like he knew something.

"I'm kind of busy, Casey. Why are you here?"

"I was hoping that in your next Dance 4 Cash—"

He held up his hand to stop her. "I'm already set with two finalists for this next contest, so . . . " He glanced at his gold watch, "One should be here any minute now to rehearse."

Josh had it all wrong. She didn't want to actually be in the competition, she had another idea. She started to explain it but her mind jumped back to what he had just said, that someone would be there soon to rehearse. Her mouth went dry. What if that someone was Chantel? "Who did you say is coming?" she asked.

"Don't worry. It's not her. New guy."

Footsteps out in the warehouse caught Josh's attention. He excused himself to go greet whoever it was.

Casey chewed on the inside of her cheek as she waited for him to return. Josh clearly said "not her." He must know about Casey and Chantel's feud. Her ex-best friend had been spreading all sorts of gossip about how terrible of a dancer she was, which was the entire reason why Casey had devised this plan and sought out Josh's help.

The new dancer was African American and looked to be about thirty. Josh and he chatted in the open warehouse for a minute, while Casey watched from the office. Josh returned shortly and inserted a USB drive into the computer; he clicked the mouse a couple times and music began to play on the warehouse speakers.

Casey and Josh watched from the office as Will owned the dance floor. He captivated them with his high energy and personal style. Casey gushed her admiration for him.

Josh agreed, said he was a sure thing, a crowd favorite. They watched Will continue to rehearse for a couple minutes in silence, until Josh gave her a quizzical look and asked, "So, what are you here for?"

Casey didn't go into great details about her situation and how Chantel's insults had shaken her confidence, but she hinted that was why she was here and needed a favor. "Let me dance as an exhibition. While everyone's waiting or whatever. Okay?" She needed for this to happen. She needed to separate herself from Chantel and show everyone—especially herself—that she had what it took to be a great dancer. She stared pleadingly at Josh.

Josh smiled softly. "Look, you're right. I know what's been going down, and I'm on your side. Honestly. But I can't. It would be bad for business. The people who come here, only come for one reason. To bet on who they believe performs the best. They come to make money on side bets, not to see an exhibition. If I let you do it, next week there will be someone else. Sorry."

Casey bowed her head and fought off tears. This crushed her. She had thought for sure Josh would let her do this.

He came over and lifted her chin so he could look her in the eyes. "You hang in there, okay?"

Back in the car, Casey slumped in the passenger seat, a scowl on her face. She didn't have to say the words for Sophia to know how the meeting went.

"Now what," Sophia asked, trying to sound upbeat. "Plan B?"

"There is no plan B," Casey said.

"I know it means a lot to you, but you'll get over it."

Casey gave her friend a side-eye smirk. There was no getting over this. She slumped lower in the seat and crossed her arms. There had to be some way to execute her plan. And then it hit her. "I'm going to do it anyway."

"You mean you're going to just walk out there and dance, even though—"

"Exactly," Casey said, defiantly. She sat upright in the car seat and gave her friend a big smile. That was exactly what she was going to do.

Concern written on her face, Sophia shook her head in disbelief and told Casey she was crazy. Then she started the car and pulled out of the parking lot, headed toward stop number two.

CHAPTER

EIGHTEEN

Sophia drove around the full parking lot until she found one of the last remaining spots at the far back edge under a Queen Palm tree. The girls grabbed their phones and headed into The School of Etiquette.

They stopped immediately inside the door, taken aback by the long line of teenage girls already waiting for their turn to enter the office door that had a sign tacked above it: Registration. They took their place at the end of the line and looked around the lobby. A water cooler stood in one corner, a hand sanitizing station placed next to a couple of chairs, and a beautiful dark wood console table adorned with a gigantic vase of fresh flowers.

For no reason at all, Sophia suddenly grabbed Casey by the shoulders, eyes-wide like she knew something but didn't want to say it, and turned Casey sharply away from the front of the line to look at the back wall of posters.

"Look! That's the one you should sign up for!" Sophia said, pointing.

Casey gave her a *what the heck is going on look* and tried to shake off Sophia's grip but Sophia would not let go. Plus she was adamant that Casey needed to read that poster right then and there. Bizarre, but Casey acquiesced to her friend's request and squinted to read the poster. "Teen Dining Table Etiquette and Formal Four Course Meal."

Had she evaded Sophia's jolting grip and been facing the front of the line mere seconds earlier she would have seen what Sophia had seen: Chantel Jackson exiting the registration office and leaving the building.

A half hour later, they were meeting Jackie Vernon Thompson. She was an attractive middle-aged Caribbean American woman dressed in a vibrant skirt suit. Her demeanor was confident and professional. She shook both girls' hands and told them to be seated.

Not thinking about where they were, Casey plopped down in her chair, her feet wide apart, like she wanted to take up as much space as possible. Sophia also plopped down but slouched and looked like she could slide off the edge of the seat at any moment. Jackie gave them a disapproving look.

"I can see I have my work cut out for me," she said. The girls looked at each other not sure what to say. Jackie asked them their names.

"I'm Sophia, but I'm not signing up."

"You do have a surname?" Jackie asked. When Sophia hesitated, Jackie clarified. "Your last name?"

Sophia told her, "Garcia."

The awkward interview continued for Casey next, who gave her first and last name and then for some reason decided to blurt, "Do you know Marquis Evans?"

Jackie stopped writing and looked at Casey. "I do not know a Marquis Evans. Why do you ask?"

Sophia flashed Casey a *don't say another word* look so Casey shook her head and said, "Never mind."

Jackie refused to never mind and pressed Casey to explain. Casey would later confess to Sophia how nervous she had been sitting in front of Jackie and when she got that nervous she had a habit of blurting things out. Which was exactly what happened as she relayed everything to Jackie about Marquis and the country club dinner with his family.

"I see," Jackie said. "I can definitely help you with such a dinner engagement. First impressions are everything, ladies. You only get one opportunity to do it right. And to be honest, my first impression of both of you leaves a lot to be desired. Fortunately, we can fix that." She handed Casey a piece of paper. "Here is an application. I sincerely hope you will fill it out. Our teen class is only a week away."

As the girls stood up to leave, Jackie handed Sophia her own application. "Please consider it. You won't be sorry. Maybe Marquis will ask you to dinner someday?" Though she remained quite serious after her comment, her eyes gave away just a hint of a smile.

Casey shook her head and said, "Not happening."

They all smiled at that.

CHAPTER

NINETEEN

The third and final stop on their itinerary for that day was close to Casey's neighborhood. Sophia pulled through a spot and parked so the car faced the opposite direction of the strip of businesses. She offered to wait, but Casey said she would walk the two blocks home. Some fresh air and exercise would do her good. They said their goodbyes and promised to call each other.

Casey took a deep breath and walked up to the door of the coffee shop, noting the "We're Hiring" sign on the front window. She patted her back pocket for her phone and realized it wasn't there. Knowing she must have left it in the car, she rushed back to the parked vehicle before Sophia could drive away. Because the car was facing away from the businesses, Sophia hadn't seen Casey running back. Casey flung open the passenger door and Sophia nearly jumped out of her seat. She had her cell phone up to her ear and when she saw Casey her eyes went wide. She told whoever was on the phone to hold on a minute and hugged the phone, screen down, against her breastbone—so Casey couldn't see the caller's name. "What's up," Sophia asked, trying to sound casual, but she looked guilty and Casey knew something was up.

Casey eyed her friend suspiciously. She grabbed her own phone off the seat, waved it at Sophia as her response, and tucked it safely into her pocket. She wanted more than anything to know why her friend was being so weird about the phone call, but didn't have time to interrogate her since her interview was starting soon. She promised to call later, to which Sophia gave a little nervous wave.

So bizarre, Casey thought as she entered the coffee shop. The warmth and aroma of fresh ground beans hit her immediately. She tried to get into the right headspace for her interview but she was preoccupied about Sophia's behavior. That was the second time that day Sophia had acted in a weird way. Earlier at the School of Etiquette she had bugged out about that poster. Something weird was going on but Casey didn't have time at the moment to figure out what. Right now she needed to land this job.

Later that evening, Casey stood in front of her bedroom mirror, checking out her new look. She thought she rocked the coffee shop apron. She started her new job in a couple days and couldn't wait to tell her mom.

After her interview she had called Sophia, who managed to evade answering Casey's questions about the weirdly timed phone call. Sophia blew it off like it was nothing important, but Casey had a feeling that wasn't true. She planned to find out what all the secrecy was about.

CHAPTER

TWENTY

A week later, Casey and Sophia, along with five other girls around their same ages, sat at a table set for eight people. Stacked in front of each girl was a dinner plate, salad plate, and soup bowl. To the left of the dishes were a small salad fork and bigger dinner fork. To the right was a dinner knife, teaspoon, and dinner spoon. Directly above the plates were a smaller fork and spoon meant for dessert. Each girl had a water glass to the top right of their plates and a bread plate to the top left. Jackie told them they were waiting on one more student.

Just then Chantel sauntered in through the door with her head down, texting. Casey, stunned, looked at Sophia, who shrugged like it wasn't a big deal. Her first instinct was to leave, but when she started to stand up, Sophia grabbed her arm and made her stay.

"Excuse me, Chantel. The rules explicitly stated cell phones are not allowed," Jackie said.

All eyes were on Chantel as she looked up, glanced around the table. Casey gave her a cold stare. Chantel spotted the empty seat and headed for it. "This must be mine."

Jackie stepped in her path and said calmly, "It was yours. Come with me, please."

Chantel muttered something under her breath but followed Jackie out of the room. The remaining girls looked around uneasily at each other as they waited for Jackie and Chantel to return.

A Better Way

Casey wondered why this kept happening, why she kept running into Chantel. Did Sophia know she was going to be there? She didn't look all that surprised when Chantel came strolling in. Casey refused to make eye contact with Sophia. She knew it wasn't right to be mad at her friend without knowing the truth, but she couldn't help feeling sorry for herself. Sophia grabbed her hand and squeezed it, but Casey ignored her.

A few moments later, Jackie returned sans Chantel. She explained to them that disruptions were bound to happen but her advice for dealing with them was "Remain calm, stay poised and let those in authority handle it." Jackie smiled warmly at each of them and the girls nodded their understanding. Casey took that advice to heart. She had already destroyed her bedroom once from anger and never wanted to feel that way again. She let any animosity drain away and chose to make the most out of the class.

They spent the rest of the day learning all about proper etiquette and how to eat a fancy four course meal.

CHAPTER

TWENTY-ONE

To any area visitors who happened to drive past the old packing plant warehouse during the day, the building looked nondescript, abandoned even. There was nothing on the outside that made one think anything of interest happened there. But if someone happened upon it on the night of a Dance 4 Cash competition, the narrative that nobody used the building anymore was immediately destroyed.

Casey and Sophia walked through the packed parking lot together. Salsa music blared from speakers. Food trucks were lined up serving tacos, burgers, and jerk wings. A huge crowd mingled and moved around. Break dancers challenged each other, stilt walkers roamed about, skate boarders zipped by. In one part of the parking lot, an impromptu car show had popped up again, drawing in a line of exotic and vintage cars, some with their hoods up. The festive chaos added excitement to the anticipation everyone felt. This crowd seemed much larger than last time, which led Casey to believe that word had gotten out about the new challenger, Will, and how he might be good enough to beat Chantel.

Thankfully, the night was slightly chilly, which meant Casey didn't look too silly wearing the ankle-length coat. She had borrowed the item from her mother's closet, needing something that would cover her outfit until she was ready to reveal it.

A Better Way

She and Sophia linked arms and headed inside the warehouse.

The neon lights flashed, cutting through the hazy fog. Undeniably there were even more people inside this time. The girls squeezed in but the large crowd was stuffed in place like crayons in a box. They could barely move, but if they didn't find a way to get closer to the dance center, Casey would never be able to enact her plan.

Josh, on the mic, warmed the crowd up with his jokes. The temperature rose higher from all the bodies. Casey started to sweat under the coat. She looked around to see if she saw Marquis or Chantel, or anyone else, but there were too many people.

The music softened and Josh tapped the microphone. "Hey guys! My spies tell me the Fire Marshall is on the way." The crowd booed and jeered. "Open those up!" He pointed to the warehouse's old loading-dock garage doors. "But make sure no one else gets in!"

When the doors went up, a refreshing gust of cool air rushed in, providing instant relief for the overheated crowd. Everyone cheered. Josh continued cracking jokes. Laughter erupted occasionally. Eventually he quieted them down and said, "Anyway, we better get rockin'. Tonight, we have last week's winner, the dazzling Chantel Jackson!..."

As the crowd cheered and clapped their support, Casey used it as an opportunity to push closer to the dance floor. Chantel noticed her and gave Casey a smirk as she danced over to give Josh a fist bump.

Josh continued with introductions. "...to face off with a virtually unknown from the Hoosier state of Indiana. Let's hear it for Will Adams!" He gave the crowd a teasing grin and quipped, "Seriously, dancing has been allowed in Indiana since last year. True story."

Will stepped out and shook Josh's hand. The crowd politely applauded, though some exchanged doubtful looks about this new contestant. Chantel sized her competition up and rolled her eyes.

"Strange dude," Sophia whispered loudly in Casey's ear. "Hate to say it, Chantel is a lock."

"Don't be so sure," Casey replied.

The music cranked up. The dance competition officially began. Up first, Chantel. As usual, she was dressed in one of her sexiest outfits. She grooved out to the center floor and worked her body with supreme confidence. The crowd loved her.

Next up, Will. The crowd had quieted down and didn't offer the same welcoming energy as they had for Chantel. But when Will started to dance, there was an obvious shockwave that traveled through the throng of onlookers. Eyes widened, jaws dropped as they watched this newcomer ignite the dance floor. Even Sophia couldn't believe it. Casey just smiled. She knew Will Adams could dance! And he very likely could win.

Chantel's confidence seemed shook as she danced her next round. She stumbled on one move, which was something Chantel never did.

On Will's next round, he intensified his routine and performed perfectly. The stunned crowd went wild. Even when the music stopped, the crowd continued to applaud and yell his name. Chantel stood off to the side with her head bowed, fists clenched.

Josh gestured for the crowd to settle. "Wow! Let's hear it for both of our great dance performances tonight." Chantel danced out to stand next to Josh. The crowd still loved her and gave a big ovation for her performance. Will waved to the crowd as he stepped out to stand next to Chantel. There was no mistaking the crowd's favorite that night. Deafening noise filled every inch of the warehouse as they cheered for Will Adams.

Josh told the crowd to hold on while he finalized the results.

Casey knew it was now or never. With Sophia's help she had coordinated a way to have her music played at the end of the competition. When she heard it blast out of the speakers on cue, she took a deep breath and dropped the ankle-length coat. Whereas last time she had worn Chantel's style of outfit to the club, this time she wore her own style, which was the complete opposite of what Chantel had on tonight.

She stepped out on the dance floor and let the music move through her body.

After a few minutes of watching her dance, the confused crowd got restless and began booing and jeering. Casey started to lose momentum. This wasn't the reaction she had anticipated. She caught Chantel's look of disdain, which would have been enough to send her off the floor in tears, except someone wearing a long coat and hat covering his face stepped out of the crowd and offered Casey his hand. Casey took it and allowed him to lead her back to the center, where the mystery person shrugged off his coat and flung his hat away.

Ekandem Essiet!

Sophia jumped up and down at the sight of him. Marquis grinned. Casey stared in shock. The crowd was stunned into silence.

To Casey, Ekandem said, "Follow my lead. We're gonna have some fun. Just be yourself."

"How did you know?" Casey asked, puzzled by this unexpected turn of events.

"Somebody called me," Ekandem said and nodded toward Sophia, who stood front row center now. It suddenly hit Casey. That must have been who Sophia was talking to the other day when Casey had unexpectedly returned to the car. Her heart swelled with friendship for Sophia. They hadn't known each other for long, but this girl had done so much to inspire Casey to believe in her true self. She threw her new bestie a kiss.

Ekandem swept her across the dance floor as she followed his lead and they had fun dancing whatever steps Ekandem offered. Casey and Ekandem's dance created a festive atmosphere as others started dancing, too. Josh looked grim as the crowd no longer paid him any attention. He decided to just hand Will the envelope of money as he was clearly the winner. Sophia made her way solo to the dance floor but was just as surprised as Casey when Will swept in and started dancing with her. Everyone was having such a fun time.

Casey didn't want this moment to stop. How lucky was she that she got to dance with Ekandem Essiet again. She recognized how much more comfortable she was in front of the crowd this time, wearing her own style of outfit, being her own fearless self. She glanced around looking for Marquis. Her heart dropped when she saw him standing off to the side talking to Chantel.

***

As everyone danced and enjoyed a fun time, Chantel Jackson stood off to the side of the dance floor, not sure how to process what just happened. She had lost the competition, which never happened to her. She was stuck watching her ex-friend Casey dance with Ekandem, not only the best choreographer in Orlando, but Chantel's mentor. *How did Casey even pull that off*, Chantel wondered. Bitterness tugged at her tongue, like she needed to say something to someone to get the taste out of her mouth. She had been good to Casey. Had taught her better dance moves, helped her dress sexier. The only reason Casey was getting any attention was because Chantel had helped make her. And how did Casey thank her? By dropping her for that weird girl Sophia! *So be it*, Chantel thought. She had other friends too. Plus she had over a million followers. Casey was nowhere close.

She saw Marquis standing by himself off to the side, watching Casey out on the dance floor. *Now was as good of a time as any to find out his deal*, she told herself.

She sashayed over to him, willing him to look at her, to want her more than he wanted anyone. No denying she looked way sexier than Casey tonight. Why wouldn't he want her?

He acknowledged her as she approached. *Off to a good start*, she thought. "Hey, I have to ask, Did I do something wrong?" She paused but he didn't offer a response, so she stepped closer and continued. "You totally ignore me, did I say something... Most guys I meet take one look and—"

"—Chantel! I'm not most guys." He took a step back from her. "Look, you're an exceptional dancer, but..." He stopped, as if thinking twice about his words.

"What? Say it," she demanded.

He looked around gathering his thoughts, then looked at her and said, "You're not someone I could take home to meet my parents."

Chantel let that statement sink in. So he couldn't let her meet his parents because...of what his parents would think of her? Which meant she wasn't the type of girl his parents approved of. Because of the way she dressed? Danced? No doubt. She understood now. What she had on offer wasn't what a guy like Marquis was looking for.

She frowned and he quickly apologized and walked away.

CHAPTER
TWENTY-TWO

The last person Casey expected to see at the dance competition was her mother. She had been enjoying herself immensely when suddenly Marquis and her mother came grooving onto the dance floor, both laughing at their attempts of doing the Vogue, a flashback to the Madonna era.

Casey did a double take. "Mom! What are you doing here?"

"Talk later. Maybe you can pick up some 90s vibe!" Her mother smiled for the first time in months; she genuinely looked like she was having a good time. Stunned, Casey watched her mother dance around like she had no other cares in the world. Any annoyance she might have felt at her mother for showing up uninvited started to give way to joy. If anyone deserved to have fun, it was her mother.

However, she still racked her brain, trying to figure out how her mother knew where to find her. Ekandem spoke up and explained he had been the one to call. He mentioned how something Sophia had said when she originally called him to set up their plan had caused him concern. He did what he thought was best for Casey's well-being and called her mom.

Casey watched her mom living in the moment and knew she couldn't be upset with her. As the dance floor filled with more dancers, Ekandem led everyone in what would turn out to be one of the best grand finales of any Dance 4 Cash competition.

CHAPTER
TWENTY-THREE

    Casey clocked in for the mid-afternoon shift at the coffee shop. She had been employed for two months now and loved the job and having her own money. Business was slow when she first arrived for her shift so she went around the shop tidying things up. Near the counter, there was a community printer customers could use for free. Casey checked the paper tray and ink levels. Then she walked around the dining area, wiping tables down, straightening chairs, picking up litter. She kept the coffee shop as clean and organized as her bedroom.

    Their only customer sat at a table in the back corner by the side exit door. The person, working on a laptop, had a hoodie pulled up blocking their face. Curious, Casey moved closer to peek at the computer screen. Some website titled "Motivational Institute for Entrepreneurs."

    The customer must have sensed Casey reading over their shoulder.

    "Excuse me!" the person said whipping around. Chantel! Both girls recognized one another at the same time.

    "Sorry," Casey said, "my bad."

    As Casey turned away, Chantel said, "Wait. You work here?"

    They chit chatted for a few minutes as Casey shared the bare minimum of her current life. Stilted and awkward, this conversation was nothing like the talks they used to enjoy as friends. Casey was sad that this was where they were now.

Just as Casey was going to excuse herself and get back to work, Chantel blurted, "Thanks!"

"Thanks? For what?" She wasn't sure if Chantel was being sarcastic or genuine.

"For your advice."

"My advice?"

"Remember that day in my bedroom, you said I would make a great choreographer? You said, 'Choreography by Chantel.'" Chantel made the same billboard in the sky gesture Casey had.

Casey remembered and told Chantel she had meant it. "You would."

"I didn't believe you then. But now I know it's something worthwhile I can offer." She fiddled with her hoodie string, lost in her thoughts for a moment. "We had a lot of bad stuff going on. And it got worse."

"What happened to us? We always got along when we were kids?"

Not wanting to or not able to answer, Chantel changed the subject. "How is he?"

"How is who?"

"Marquis."

"Oh, last time I saw him . . . Was over two months ago." Casey still liked him, but she needed to deal with everything that had happened in her life the last few months; both she and Marquis had decided to take their friendship—and whatever else might develop—slow for now. "His parents invited me—"

"—Right. His parents." Chantel smirked and looked like she was going to add some context, but the coffee shop door chimed and an elderly man entered, breaking their conversation.

Casey told Chantel she'd be right back and hustled over to help the customer.

She took the gentleman's order, which should have been quick and easy to fill but turned out to be anything but. When she dropped off his pastry the elderly man realized he had ordered the wrong thing. He needed a couple minutes to look through the options in the display case before he decided his second choice. While fixing his latte, she accidentally dropped the cup, spilling coffee all over the floor. Mopping, which had to be done immediately, added an extra several minutes to her task of helping this one customer. After she handed the gentleman his new cup of coffee, she finally rushed to the back of the shop, hoping to pick up the conversation where they had left it, but Chantel and all her belongings were gone.

Disappointed, Casey headed back to her station, passing the community printer. There was a sheet on the output tray. Since she had tidied this area up when she first clocked into work she knew this sheet was new. She grabbed the piece of paper and read.

It had printed out as letterhead for the Motivational Institute. A project was listed: Choreography by Chantel. Casey smiled at that.

>Hey Casey,
>Couldn't wait. No. That's not true. Easier this way. Guess I don't have it in me to apologize face to face. I can't explain what got into me. I was so pissed off. I became this mean and ugly person who wanted to hurt you. I'm so sorry.
>Marquis was part of it. If I couldn't have him, then I wanted to make sure you couldn't either.
>I ended up hating myself. I don't deserve forgiveness. First, I have to learn to forgive myself, and I'm not there yet.
>I have a lot of work to do before I can even respect who I am again. There has to be a better way. I hope I find it.

Casey folded the sheet of paper and tucked it into her apron pocket. She wasn't sure if she and Chantel would ever be besties again, but at least maybe they could be friends. This was a start. She was proud of Chantel for taking a chance, for believing in herself, and having the guts to start her own choreography business. She appreciated what

Chantel had said about finding a better way. Casey had found her own better way, and she knew, deep in her soul, that Chantel would find hers too.

www.ingramcontent.com/pod-product-compliance
Lightning Source LLC
Chambersburg PA
CBHW031604040426
42452CB00006B/403